Reading & Writing
LESSONS FOR THE SMART BOARD™

Motivating, Interactive Lessons That Teach
Key Reading & Writing Skills

SCHOLASTIC

New York ○ Toronto ○ London ○ Auckland ○ Sydney
New Delhi ○ Mexico City ○ Hong Kong ○ Buenos Aires

Teaching Resources

Authors: Rachel Ager (K), Julia Rutherford-Bate (K), Karen Mawer (Gr. 1), Heather Cromie (Gr. 1)
Illustrators: Jim Peacock (Notebook file illustrations), Jenny Tulip (book and additional Notebook file illustrations),
Theresa Tibbetts (additional Notebook file illustrations)
Editor: Maria L. Chang
Cover design: Brian LaRossa
Interior design: Grafica Inc.

CD-ROM developed in association with Q & D Multimedia

Special thanks to Robin Hunt and Melissa Rugless of Scholastic Ltd.

SMART Board™ and Notebook™ are registered trademarks of SMART Technologies Inc.
Microsoft Office, Word, and Excel are either registered trademarks or trademarks of Microsoft Corporation in the United States and/or other countries.

All Flash activities designed and developed by Q & D Multimedia.

The publishers gratefully acknowledge:
The Peters, Fraser and Dunlop Group for the use of an extract from *We're going on a bear hunt* by Michael Rosen © 1993, Michael Rosen (1993, Walker Books).

Contents

Introduction

Interactive whiteboards are fast becoming the must-have resource in today's classroom as they allow teachers to facilitate children's learning in ways that were inconceivable a few years ago. The appropriate use of interactive whiteboards, whether used daily in the classroom or once a week in a computer lab, encourages active participation in lessons and increases students' determination to succeed. Interactive whiteboards make it easier for teachers to bring subjects across the curriculum to life in new and exciting ways.

What can an interactive whiteboard offer?

For teachers, an interactive whiteboard allows them to do the same things they can on an ordinary whiteboard, such as drawing, writing, and erasing. However, the interactive whiteboard also offers many other possibilities, such as:

- saving any work created during a lesson;
- preparing as many pages as necessary;
- displaying any page within the Notebook™ file to review teaching and learning;
- adding scanned examples of the children's work to a Notebook file;
- changing colors of shapes and backgrounds instantly;
- using simple templates and grids;
- linking Notebook files to spreadsheets, Web sites, and presentations.

Using an interactive whiteboard in the simple ways outlined above can enrich teaching and learning in a classroom, but that is only the beginning of the whiteboard's potential to educate and inspire.

For students, the interactive whiteboard provides the opportunity to share learning experiences, as lessons can be delivered with sound, still and moving images, and Web sites. Interactive whiteboards can be used to cater to the needs of all learning styles:

- Kinesthetic learners benefit from being able to physically manipulate images.
- Visual learners benefit from being able to watch videos, look at photographs, and see images being manipulated.
- Auditory learners benefit from being able to access audio resources, such as voice recordings and sound effects.

With a little preparation, all of these resource types could be integrated into one lesson—a feat that would have been almost impossible before the advent of the interactive whiteboard!

Access to an interactive whiteboard

In schools where students have limited access to an interactive whiteboard, carefully planned lessons will help students get the most benefit from it during the times they can use it. As teachers become familiar with the interactive whiteboard, they will learn when to use it and, equally important, when not to use it!

Where permanent access to an interactive whiteboard is available, it is important to plan the use of the board effectively. It should be used only in ways that will enhance or extend teaching and learning. Children still need to gain practical, first-hand experience of many things. Some experiences cannot be recreated on an interactive whiteboard, but others cannot be had without it. *Reading & Writing Lessons for the SMART Board™* offers both teachers and learners the most accessible and creative uses of this most valuable resource.

About the book

Adapted from Scholastic UK's best-selling 100 SMART Board™ Lessons series, *Reading & Writing Lessons for the SMART Board™* is designed to reflect best practice in using interactive whiteboards. It is also designed to support all teachers in using this valuable tool by providing lessons and other resources that can be used on the SMART Board with little or no preparation. These inspirational lessons meet the English language arts Common Core State Standards and are perfect for all levels of experience.

This book is divided into three chapters. Each chapter contains lessons covering:

- Reading & Phonics
- Writing
- Capitalization & Punctuation

Mini-Lessons

The mini-lessons have a consistent structure that includes:

- a **Getting Started** activity;
- a step-by-step **Mini-Lesson** plan;
- an **Independent Work** activity; and
- a **Wrap-Up** activity to round up the teaching and learning and identify any assessment opportunities.

Each mini-lesson identifies any resources required (including Notebook files that are provided on the CD-ROM, as well as reproducible activity pages) and lists the whiteboard tools that could be used in the mini-lesson.

The reproducible activity sheets toward the back of the book support the mini-lessons. These sheets provide opportunities for group or individual work to be completed away from the board, while linking to the context of the whiteboard lesson. They also provide opportunities for whole-class discussions in which children present their work.

What's on the CD-ROM?

The accompanying CD-ROM provides an extensive bank of Notebook files designed for use with the SMART Board. These support, and are supported by, the mini-lessons in this book. They can be annotated and saved for reference or for use with subsequent lessons; they can also be printed out. In addition to texts and images, a selection of Notebook files include the following types of files:

- **Embedded Microsoft Word files:** The embedded files are launched from the Notebook file and will open in their native Microsoft application.

- **Embedded interactive files:** These include specially commissioned interactive files that will open in a new browser window within the Notebook environment.

- **Embedded audio files:** Some Notebook files contain buttons that play sounds.

- **"Build Your Own" file:** This contains a blank Notebook page with a bank of selected images and interactive tools from the Gallery, as well as specially commissioned images. You can use this to help build your own Notebook files.

The Notebook files

All of the Notebook files have a consistent structure as follows:

- **Title and objectives page**—Use this page to highlight the focus of the mini-lesson. You might also wish to refer to this page at certain times throughout the lesson or at the end of the lesson to assess whether the learning objective was achieved.

- **Getting Started activity**—This sets the context to the lesson and usually provides some key questions or learning points that will be addressed through the main activities.

- **Main activities**—These activities offer independent, collaborative group, or whole-class work. The activities draw on the full scope of Notebook software and the associated tools, as well as the SMART Board tools. "What to Do" boxes are also included in many of the prepared Notebook files. These appear as tabs in the top right-hand corner of the screen. To access these notes, simply pull out the tabs to reveal planning information, additional support, and key learning points.

- **Wrap-Up**—A whole-class activity or summary page is designed to review work done both at the board and away from the board. In many lessons, children are encouraged to present their work.

How to Use the CD-ROM

Setting up your screen for optimal use

It is best to view the Notebook pages at a screen display setting of 1280 x 1024 pixels. To alter the screen display, select Settings, then Control Panel from the Start menu. Next, double-click on the Display icon, then click on the Settings tab. Finally, adjust the Screen area scroll bar to 1280 x 1024 pixels. Click on OK. (On the Mac, click on the apple icon and select System Preferences. Then click on Displays and select 1280 x 1024.)

If you prefer to use a screen display setting of 800 x 600 pixels, ensure that your Notebook view is set to "Page Width." To alter the view, launch Notebook and click on View. Go to Zoom and select the "Page Width" setting. If you use a screen display setting of 800 x 600 pixels, text in the prepared Notebook files may appear larger when you edit it on screen.

Getting started

The program should run automatically when you insert the CD-ROM into your CD drive. If it does not, use My Computer to browse to the contents of the CD-ROM and click on the Scholastic icon. (On the Mac, click on the Scholastic icon to start the program.)

Main menu

The Main menu divides the Notebook files by topic: Reading & Phonics; Writing; and Capitalization & Punctuation. Clicking on the appropriate button for any of these options will take you to a separate Lessons menu. (See below for further information.) The "Build Your Own" file is also accessed through the Main menu.

Individual Notebook files or pages can be located using the search facility by keying in words (or part of words) from the resource titles in the Search box. Press Go to begin the search. This will bring up a list of the titles that match your search.

Lessons menu

Each Lessons menu provides all of the prepared Notebook files for each chapter of the book. Click on the buttons to open the Notebook files. Click on Main menu button to return to the Main menu screen. (To alternate between the menus on the CD-ROM and other open applications, hold down the Alt key and press the Tab key to switch to the desired application.)

Safety note: Avoid looking directly at the projector beam as it is potentially damaging to the eyes, and never leave children unsupervised when using the interactive whiteboard.

Connections to the Common Core State Standards

The mini-lessons and activities in this book meet the following Common Core State Standards for English Language Arts:

READING & PHONICS	
Print Around the Classroom	**RF.K.1 and RF.1.1:** Demonstrate understanding of the organization and basic features or print. **RF.K.1a:** Follow words from left to right, top to bottom, and page by page. **RF.K.1b:** Recognize that spoken words are represented in written language by specific sequences of letters. **RF.K.2 and RF.1.2:** Demonstrate understanding of spoken words, syllables, and sounds. **RF.K.4:** Read emergent-reader texts with purpose and understanding. **RF.1.4a:** Read on-level text with purpose and understanding.
Print All Around Us	**RF.K.1 and RF.1.1:** Demonstrate understanding of the organization and basic features or print. **RF.K.1a:** Follow words from left to right, top to bottom, and page by page. **RF.K.1b:** Recognize that spoken words are represented in written language by specific sequences of letters. **RF.K.2 and RF.1.2:** Demonstrate understanding of spoken words, syllables, and sounds. **RF.K.4:** Read emergent-reader texts with purpose and understanding. **RF.1.4a:** Read on-level text with purpose and understanding.
Letter Sounds	**RF.K.3a:** Demonstrate basic knowledge of one-to-one letter-sound correspondences by producing the primary or many of the most frequent sound for each consonant.
Bear Hunt	**RL.K.2:** With prompting and support, retell familiar stories, including key details. **RL.K.3:** With prompting and support, identify characters, settings, and major events in a story. **RL.K.7:** With prompting and support, describe the relationship between illustrations and the story in which they appear. **RL.K.10:** Actively engage in group reading activities with purpose and understanding. **RL.1.2:** Retell stories, including key details, and demonstrate understanding of their central message or lesson. **RL.1.3:** Describe characters, settings, and major events in a story, using key details. **RL.1.7:** Use illustrations and details in a story to describe its characters, setting, or events. **RL.1.10:** With prompting and support, read prose and poetry of appropriate complexity for grade 1.
Memory Game	**RF.K.3a:** Demonstrate basic knowledge of one-to-one letter-sound correspondences by producing the primary or many of the most frequent sound for each consonant.
Goldilocks's Story	**RL.K.2:** With prompting and support, retell familiar stories, including key details. **RL.K.3:** With prompting and support, identify characters, settings, and major events in a story. **RL.K.7:** With prompting and support, describe the relationship between illustrations and the story in which they appear. **RL.K.10:** Actively engage in group reading activities with purpose and understanding. **RL.1.2:** Retell stories, including key details, and demonstrate understanding of their central message or lesson. **RL.1.3:** Describe characters, settings, and major events in a story, using key details. **RL.1.7:** Use illustrations and details in a story to describe its characters, setting, or events. **RL.1.10:** With prompting and support, read prose and poetry of appropriate complexity for grade 1.
Word Circle Game	**RF.K.2c:** Blend and segment onsets and rimes of single-syllable spoken words. **RF.K.2d:** Isolate and pronounce the initial, medial vowel, and final sounds (phonemes) in three-phoneme (CVC) words. **RF.K.2e:** Add or substitute individual sounds (phonemes) in simple, one-syllable words to make new words. **RF.1.2c:** Isolate and pronounce the initial, medial vowel, and final sounds (phonemes) in spoken single-syllable words. **RF.1.2d:** Segment spoken single-syllable words into their complete sequence of individual sounds (phonemes).
Rhyming Game	**RF.K.2a:** Recognize and produce rhyming words. **RF.K.2c:** Blend and segment onsets and rimes of single-syllable spoken words. **RF.K.2d:** Isolate and pronounce the initial, medial vowel, and final sounds (phonemes) in three-phoneme (CVC) words. **RF.K.2e:** Add or substitute individual sounds (phonemes) in simple, one-syllable words to make new words. **RF.1.2c:** Isolate and pronounce the initial, medial vowel, and final sounds (phonemes) in spoken single-syllable words. **RF.1.2d:** Segment spoken single-syllable words into their complete sequence of individual sounds (phonemes).

Making Words	**RF.K.2c:** Blend and segment onsets and rimes of single-syllable spoken words. **RF.K.2d:** Isolate and pronounce the initial, medial vowel, and final sounds (phonemes) in three-phoneme (CVC) words. **RF.1.2c:** Isolate and pronounce the initial, medial vowel, and final sounds (phonemes) in spoken single-syllable words. **RF.1.2d:** Segment spoken single-syllable words into their complete sequence of individual sounds (phonemes).
Robotic Words	**RF.K.2c:** Blend and segment onsets and rimes of single-syllable spoken words. **RF.K.2d:** Isolate and pronounce the initial, medial vowel, and final sounds (phonemes) in three-phoneme (CVC) words. **RF.1.2c:** Isolate and pronounce the initial, medial vowel, and final sounds (phonemes) in spoken single-syllable words. **RF.1.2d:** Segment spoken single-syllable words into their complete sequence of individual sounds (phonemes).
Words That Rhyme	**RF.K.2a:** Recognize and produce rhyming words.
CVC Words, Part 1	**RF.K.2d:** Isolate and pronounce the initial, medial vowel, and final sounds (phonemes) in three-phoneme (CVC) words. **RF.K.2e:** Add or substitute individual sounds (phonemes) in simple, one-syllable words to make new words. **RF.1.2c:** Isolate and pronounce the initial, medial vowel, and final sounds (phonemes) in spoken single-syllable words.
CVC Words, Part 2	**RF.K.2d:** Isolate and pronounce the initial, medial vowel, and final sounds (phonemes) in three-phoneme (CVC) words. **RF.K.2e:** Add or substitute individual sounds (phonemes) in simple, one-syllable words to make new words. **RF.1.2c:** Isolate and pronounce the initial, medial vowel, and final sounds (phonemes) in spoken single-syllable words.
Color Words	**RF.K.3:** Know and apply grade-level phonics and word analysis skills in decoding words. **RF.1.3g:** Recognize and read grade-appropriate irregularly spelled words. **L.1.5a:** Sort words into categories (e.g., colors) to gain a sense of the concepts the categories represent.
Reading High-Frequency Words	**RF.K.3c:** Read common high-frequency words by sight. **RF.1.3g:** Recognize and read grade-appropriate irregularly spelled words.
Initial Consonant Blends, Part 1	**RF.1.3a:** Know the spelling-sound correspondences for common consonant digraphs.
Initial Consonant Blends, Part 2	**RF.1.3a:** Know the spelling-sound correspondences for common consonant digraphs.
Ending Consonant Blends	**RF.1.3a:** Know the spelling-sound correspondences for common consonant digraphs.
Spelling High-Frequency Words	**RF.1.3g:** Recognize and read grade-appropriate irregularly spelled words.
Missing Words	**L.K.6 and L.1.6:** Use words and phrases acquired through conversations, reading and being read to, and responding to texts.
Long-e Vowel Sound	**RF.K.3b:** Associate the long and short sounds with common spellings (graphemes) for the five major vowels. **RF.1.2a:** Distinguish long from short vowel sounds in spoken single-syllable words. **RF.1.3c:** Know final –e and common vowel team conventions for representing long vowel sounds.
Long-o Vowel Sound	**RF.K.3b:** Associate the long and short sounds with common spellings (graphemes) for the five major vowels. **RF.1.2a:** Distinguish long from short vowel sounds in spoken single-syllable words. **RF.1.3c:** Know final –e and common vowel team conventions for representing long vowel sounds.
/oo/ Vowel Sound	**RF.K.3b:** Associate the long and short sounds with common spellings (graphemes) for the five major vowels. **RF.1.2a:** Distinguish long from short vowel sounds in spoken single-syllable words.
Silent e	**RF.1.3c:** Know final –e and common vowel team conventions for representing long vowel sounds.
Reading Nonfiction	**RI.K.1:** With prompting and support, ask and answer questions about key details in a text. **RI.K.2:** With prompting and support, identify the main topic and retell key details of a text. **RI.K.5:** Identify the front cover, back cover, and title page of a book. **RI.K.10:** Actively engage in group reading activities with purpose and understanding. **RI.1.1:** Ask and answer questions about key details in a text. **RI.1.2:** Identify the main topic and retell key details of a text. **RI.1.5:** Know and use various text features (e.g., headings, tables of contents, glossaries, electronic menus, icons) to locate key facts and information in a text.

WRITING

Listening to Narratives	**SL.K.2:** Confirm understanding of a text read aloud or information presented orally or through other media by asking and answering questions about key details and requesting clarification if something is not understood. **SL.1.2:** Ask and answer questions about key details in a text read aloud or information presented orally or through other media.
Writing Captions	**W.K.2:** Use a combination of drawing, dictating, and writing to compose informative/explanatory texts in which they name what they are writing about and supply some information about the topic. **W.K.6 and W.1.6:** With guidance and support from adults, explore/use a variety of digital tools to produce and publish writing, including in collaboration with peers. **W.K.7 and W.1.7:** Participate in shared research and writing projects. **W.1.2:** Write informative/explanatory texts in which they name a topic, supply some facts about the topic, and provide some sense of closure.

Greeting Cards	**W.K.7 and W.1.7:** Participate in shared research and writing projects. **L.K.5c and L.1.5c:** Identify real-life connections between words and their use. **L.K.6:** Use words and phrases acquired through conversations, reading and being read to, and responding to texts.
Writing With Purpose	**W.K.7 and W.1.7:** Participate in shared research and writing projects. **L.K.1f:** Produce and expand complete sentences in shared language activities. **L.K.5c and L.1.5c:** Identify real-life connections between words and their use. **L.K.6:** Use words and phrases acquired through conversations, reading and being read to, and responding to texts.
Sequencing	**W.K.3:** Use a combination of drawing, dictating, and writing to narrate a single event or several loosely linked events, tell about the events in the order in which they occurred, and provide a reaction to what happened. **W.K.6 and W.1.6:** With guidance and support from adults, explore/use a variety of digital tools to produce and publish writing, including in collaboration with peers. **W.K.7 and W.1.7:** Participate in shared research and writing projects. **W.1.3:** Write narratives in which they recount two or more appropriately sequenced events, include some details regarding what happened, use temporal words to signal event order, and provide some sense of closure. **L.K.1f:** Produce and expand complete sentences in shared language activities.
Writing Directions	**W.K.3:** Use a combination of drawing, dictating, and writing to narrate a single event or several loosely linked events, tell about the events in the order in which they occurred, and provide a reaction to what happened. **W.K.6 and W.1.6:** With guidance and support from adults, explore/use a variety of digital tools to produce and publish writing, including in collaboration with peers. **W.K.7 and W.1.7:** Participate in shared research and writing projects. **W.1.3:** Write narratives in which they recount two or more appropriately sequenced events, include some details regarding what happened, use temporal words to signal event order, and provide some sense of closure. **L.K.1f:** Produce and expand complete sentences in shared language activities.
Captions	**W.K.2:** Use a combination of drawing, dictating, and writing to compose informative/explanatory texts in which they name what they are writing about and supply some information about the topic. **W.K.6 and W.1.6:** With guidance and support from adults, explore/use a variety of digital tools to produce and publish writing, including in collaboration with peers. **W.K.7 and W.1.7:** Participate in shared research and writing projects. **L.K.1 and L.1.1:** Demonstrate command of the conventions of standard English grammar and usage when writing or speaking. **L.K.1f:** Produce and expand complete sentences in shared language activities.
Making a List	**W.K.2:** Use a combination of drawing, dictating, and writing to compose informative/explanatory texts in which they name what they are writing about and supply some information about the topic. **W.K.6 and W.1.6:** With guidance and support from adults, explore/use a variety of digital tools to produce and publish writing, including in collaboration with peers. **W.K.7 and W.1.7:** Participate in shared research and writing projects. **L.K.1 and L.1.1:** Demonstrate command of the conventions of standard English grammar and usage when writing or speaking.
Plurals	**L.K.1c:** Form regular plural nouns by adding /s/ or /es/.
Design a Superhero	**W.K.6 and W.1.6:** With guidance and support from adults, explore/use a variety of digital tools to produce and publish writing, including in collaboration with peers. **W.K.7 and W.1.7:** Participate in shared research and writing projects. **L.K.1f:** Produce and expand complete sentences in shared language activities.
Retelling a Story	**W.K.3:** Use a combination of drawing, dictating, and writing to narrate a single event or several loosely linked events, tell about the events in the order in which they occurred, and provide a reaction to what happened. **W.K.6 and W.1.6:** With guidance and support from adults, explore/use a variety of digital tools to produce and publish writing, including in collaboration with peers. **W.K.7 and W.1.7:** Participate in shared research and writing projects. **W.1.3:** Write narratives in which they recount two or more appropriately sequenced events, include some details regarding what happened, use temporal words to signal event order, and provide some sense of closure. **L.K.1f:** Produce and expand complete sentences in shared language activities.
Describing Things	**W.K.2:** Use a combination of drawing, dictating, and writing to compose informative/explanatory texts in which they name what they are writing about and supply some information about the topic. **W.K.6 and W.1.6:** With guidance and support from adults, explore/use a variety of digital tools to produce and publish writing, including in collaboration with peers. **W.K.7 and W.1.7:** Participate in shared research and writing projects. **W.1.2:** Write informative/explanatory texts in which they name a topic, supply some facts about the topic, and provide some sense of closure.

CAPITALIZATION & PUNCTUATION

Capital Letters	**L.K.1a:** Print many upper- and lowercase letters. **L.K.2a:** Capitalize the first word in a sentence and the pronoun *I*. **L.1.1a:** Print all upper- and lowercase letters.
Periods	**L.K.2b:** Recognize and name end punctuation. **L.1.2b:** Use end punctuation for sentences.
Question Marks	**L.K.2b:** Recognize and name end punctuation. **L.1.2b:** Use end punctuation for sentences.

Print Around the Classroom

Learning objectives

- To use talk to connect ideas.
- To use talk to organize, sequence, and clarify thinking.
- To know that print carries meaning.

Resources

- "Print Around the Classroom" Notebook file
- "Classroom Labels" (p. 57)
- digital camera

Whiteboard tools

- Pen tray
- Highlighter pen
- Lines tool
- Select tool

Getting Started

Discuss with children what they do in different areas of the classroom. Ask: *What do we do in this area? Where do we hang up our coats? Where can we get a drink?*

Highlight the labels on page 2 of the "Print Around the Classroom" Notebook file and link them to those that already exist around the classroom. Ask: *What are these? What do you think this label says? What else could it say? Who or what are the labels for?*

Mini-Lesson

1. Display page 3 of the Notebook file. Read the label aloud and then demonstrate that you can press on the label to listen to the words being read.

2. Ask: *Which picture do you think the label belongs to? Why have you chosen that picture? Could the label work with any other pictures?*

3. Allow children plenty of time to talk to their friends and think about their answers. Encourage them to explain their answers. Ask: *Why? Why not?*

4. Use the Lines tool to draw an arrow on page 3 to identify which picture children think best matches the label. They can check if their answer is correct by pressing on the relevant picture to hear the label read aloud.

5. Look at the remaining pictures on the page and discuss why the label might not match them.

6. Repeat the activity using pages 4 to 8.

Independent Work

Write your own labels or use "Classroom Labels" (p. 57). Cut out the labels and give one to each pair of children. Invite them to take a digital photograph to go with each label. Alternatively, ask children to choose an area in the classroom where the label might be displayed.

Wrap-Up

Refer back to the labels around the room that children looked at earlier. Can they think of any places in the room that need a label? Ask: *What labels can we think of to put around the room?* If time is available, make some labels on the SMART Board, print them, and attach them to the places suggested by children.

Print All Around Us

Learning objectives
- To ascribe meanings to marks that they see in different places.
- To write their own names and other things such as labels and captions.

Resources
- "Print All Around Us" Notebook file
- "What's in Our Classroom?" (p. 58)
- collection of photographs or pictures from magazines
- pens, pencils, blank labels

Whiteboard tools
- Pen tray
- On-screen Keyboard
- Select tool

Getting Started

Review the previous lesson (Print Around the Classroom) and ask children to point out labels that exist around the classroom. Ask: *What are the labels for? What do they say? What other labels do you know?*

Compare the pictorial and textual labels that children might see. Display the labels on page 2 of the "Print All Around Us" Notebook file. Ask: *What does the picture mean? What does the writing mean?* Encourage children to think about the purpose of the labels: *Who are they for? What are they trying to say?*

Mini-Lesson

1. Go to page 3 of the Notebook file. Invite children to tell you what they can see. Ask: *What kind of label do you think we could put near the door?*

2. Give children time to talk in pairs and decide on an idea for a label.

3. Ask them to share their ideas and discuss them. Ask: *Why would that be a good label? Who do you think would like to read that label?*

4. As a class, decide on the label. Then use a Pen from the Pen tray or the On-screen Keyboard to write the label into the empty box. Read the label aloud together.

5. Repeat the activity on page 4.

Independent Work

Take your own photographs or use the pictures from "What's in Our Classroom?" (p. 58). Cut out the pictures and give each child a picture (or collection of pictures). Set up a label-making area with pens, pencils, and blank labels for children to write on. Ask them to write labels to go with the pictures you have given them.

Allow children to use Notebook pages 5 to 9 with appropriate levels of support. Encourage them to try to write inside the label space provided.

Wrap-Up

Invite children to read out their labels without telling the other children what their purpose might be. The other children should then try to guess where the label might be placed. Can they explain why they decided on particular labels? Ask: *Why did you choose that label? Who is your label for?* Use page 10 of the Notebook file to write up children's comments.

Letter Sounds

Learning objectives

- To hear and say the initial sound in words and know which letters represent some of the sounds.
- To link sounds to letters, naming and sounding the letters of the alphabet.

Resources

- "Letter Sounds" Notebook file
- "Alphabet" (p. 59)
- a large bag containing small objects, such as an apple, ball, pencil, and toy
- tape recorder
- paper
- glue
- scissors
- pencils
- crayons

Whiteboard tools

- Pen tray
- Highlighter pen
- Delete button
- Select tool
- Gallery

Getting Started

Prepare a bag with several small objects inside, such as an apple, a ball, a pencil, and so on. Pull out each object in turn. Ask children to make the initial sound of the name of each object. For example, pull out an apple and encourage children to make the sound /a/. Use page 2 of the "Letter Sounds" Notebook file to write the names of the objects as you remove them from the bag. Add images from the Gallery to go with each object if they are available.

Vary the game by giving children clues about the object before you show it. For example, say: *I begin with a. I am red and round and tasty to eat. I am a fruit. What am I?* (An apple)

Mini-Lesson, Part 1

1. Go to page 3 of the Notebook file. Ask children to make the sound of the letter *s* in the middle of the page. Press on the letter to hear the sound.

2. Practice making the sound with children. Ask them to draw the letter in the air with their finger. Trace the letter on the SMART Board with a Highlighter pen at the same time.

3. Look at the pictures on page 3. Invite children to think about the initial sound of each word.

4. Ask: *Can you see any pictures that begin with* s? Draw lines to match the pictures with the letter *s*. Suggest that the other pictures should be deleted.

5. Invite volunteers to come and delete the unwanted pictures. Ask them why they chose those particular pictures.

6. Repeat with pages 4 to 8.

Mini-Lesson, Part 2

1. For the next session, open pages 9 to 14 of the Notebook file. These contain a greater, more complex collection of choices for children to work with.

2. For each page, ask children to make the sound of the letter on the page. Press on the letter to hear the sound. Practice making the sound together and writing it in the air.

3. Next, look at and discuss the pictures that are displayed on the page. Encourage children to think about what sound they begin with. Ask: *Can you see any pictures that begin with the letter ___? Which pictures shall we delete? Why?*

4. Ask children to give reasons why some pictures might stay. For example, they may wish to keep the cake on the *h* page as it might be a "Happy Birthday" cake. Others may wish to keep the face on the *s* page because they see a smile!

5. Use a tape recorder and record a letter sound. Invite children to spend time collecting items that match the initial sound that they hear when they play the sound.

(continued)

6. Start a game and invite children to join you. Say: *My mother went to the store and bought a cake.* Explain that mother must buy things that begin with the same initial letter sound. Tell children that for the first round of the game, they must think of objects beginning with *c*.

7. Go to page 15 of the Notebook file. Invite children to use this page to make a list of their items if they so wish.

8. Show them how to use the Gallery to find any suitable pictures of the suggested items to add to the list.

Independent Work

In the workshop or writing area, create opportunities for children to make alphabet books. Provide homemade books with a letter on each page (in alphabetical order). Laminate copies of "Alphabet" (p. 59) for reference and to remind children of all the letters of the alphabet.

Wrap-Up

Pick up your bag of objects again. Tell children that you have something in your bag beginning with *b*, for example. Ask them to think of all the things that you might have beginning with *b*. Bring out your item to see if anyone has guessed correctly. Invite individuals to take turns to feel something inside the bag and then give clues to describe the object to the other children, including what letter it begins with. Review children's work and make some alphabetical word lists on page 16 of the Notebook file.

Bear Hunt

Learning objectives
- To hear some favorite stories, rhymes, songs, poems, or jingles.
- To begin to be aware of the way stories are structured.
- To know that information can be retrieved from books and computers.
- To explore and experiment with sounds, words, and texts.

Resources
- Copies of *We're Going on a Bear Hunt* by Michael Rosen (Little Simon, 1989)
- "Bear Hunt" Notebook file
- "Bear Hunt Map" (p. 60)
- action figures and vehicles
- digital camera

Whiteboard tools
- Pen tray
- Select tool
- Lines tool
- Delete button

Getting Started

Read the story *We're Going on a Bear Hunt* by Michael Rosen. Encourage children to join in with suitable actions as the family in the book journeys through different places. Suggest that children also make appropriate noises to represent the different settings: *swishy swashy*, and so on.

Look at pages 2 to 8 of the Notebook file. Press on the words at the top of each page to hear them read aloud, and listen to the sounds by pressing on the sound words.

Mini-Lesson, Part 1

1. Display page 9 of the Notebook file. Look at the story map with all the different places the family visited. Ask children to point out the different areas. Press on the labels to hear them read out.

2. Ask: *Can you remember where the family went first? Where did they go next?* Use the Lines tool to draw arrows to show the direction in which the family went.

3. As you get to each area, ask children if they can remember the sounds made, such as *swishy swashy*, and so on.

Mini-Lesson, Part 2

1. For the next session, go to page 10. Work with one group at a time. This time, ask children to change the order of the story. Invite them to drag the images into positions of their choice on the map. Press on the labels to hear them read out. (To move the labels without activating the sound labels, simply press and drag them into position.)

2. Explain to children that they do not have to use all the images if they don't want to. Use the Delete button to delete these if necessary.

3. Use the arrows provided on the page to link the images. Alternatively, you can draw your own arrows using a Pen from the Pen tray or the Lines tool.

4. When the story map is complete, invite children to retell the story with the actions and the sounds. Invite the other children to listen to this special retelling.

Independent Work

Provide children with copies of the "Bear Hunt Map" (p. 60, enlarged to 11" x 17" size), and suggest that they use the map to retell the story. Encourage them to use props such as action figures and objects to enhance their play and suggest that they make up noises and actions to accompany their storytelling.

Encourage some dramatic-play activities. Invite children to go on their own bear hunt around the classroom or outside. Ask: *Where are you going? What noises will you make?* Give children a digital camera so that they can collect images of the different places they visit. Note whether children use the materials for telling their own version of the bear hunt story, or if they develop their ideas in another way.

(continued)

Wrap-Up

Invite children who went on their own bear hunt around the classroom to share their journey with the rest of the class. Scan any digital pictures that children took and display these on page 11 of the Notebook file. (Upload digital images of children's bear hunts by selecting Insert, then Picture File, and browsing to where you have saved the images.) Encourage children to use the photographs of their bear hunt as reminders of what they did on their journey. Support children in their presentation of their bear hunt by asking questions such as: *Where did you go? What was the scariest part of your journey? Why was it scary?* Encourage the rest of the class to ask questions.

Memory Game

Learning objectives

- To hear and say the initial sound in words and know which letters represent some of the sounds.
- To interact with others, negotiating plans and activities and taking turns in conversation.
- To hear and say sounds in words in the order in which they occur.

Resources

- "Memory Game" Notebook file

Whiteboard tools

- Pen tray
- Select tool
- Screen Shade
- Gallery

Getting Started

Open page 2 of the "Memory Game" Notebook file. Ask children to look carefully at all the items on the page. Tell them to try to remember everything they can see.

Enable the Screen Shade to hide the objects. Ask: *What can you remember seeing on the page?* Go to page 3 and write the names of the objects children can remember. Sound out the words as you write them, encouraging children to join in with any sounds that they can hear, especially the initial sounds.

Now go back to page 2. Reveal the items on the page slowly. Ask: *What is this? A coat? Who remembered there was a coat on the page?* Check the list you have written on page 3 to see if the word *coat* appears on it.

Mini-Lesson

1. Go to page 4 of the Notebook file. Ask children to look carefully at the objects on the page and try to remember everything.

2. Use the Screen Shade to hide all the objects. Ask: *What can you remember seeing on the page?*

3. As children start to remember, use page 5 to write down the words.

4. Sound out the words as you write them, asking questions such as: *What sound does egg begin with?*

5. Now return to page 4 and slowly reveal the items. Ask: *What is this? A banana? Who remembered there was a banana on the page?* Check your list on page 5 to see if the word *banana* appears on it.

6. Repeat the activity on pages 6 to 9.

Independent Work

Go to page 10 of the Notebook file. Help children use the Gallery to build their own page of items on the SMART Board to play a memory game. Subsequent groups of children can use blank Notebook pages to create their memory games. Differentiate this task by setting a particular challenge—perhaps by specifying that all the items should begin with the sound /m/, or that all the items should be blue. Show children how to navigate through the images and how to drag the pictures onto the page. Demonstrate how to use the Screen Shade to hide and reveal the images. Ask questions such as: *Why have you chosen these pictures?*

Wrap-Up

Display page 10 of the Notebook file, showing one of the groups' own page that they generated during independent work. Support children who made this page to lead the memory game with the class. Allow children time to look at the page and then remove an item while they close their eyes. Ask them which object is missing. Invite volunteers to find it in the Gallery.

Goldilocks's Story

Learning objectives

- To retell narratives in the correct sequence, drawing on language patterns of stories.
- To read a range of familiar and common words and simple sentences independently.
- To show an understanding of the elements of stories, such as main character, sequence of events, and openings.

Resources

- "Goldilocks's Story" Notebook file
- "Make Your Own Story" (p. 61)
- an art area stocked with paper, pencils, crayons, glue, and scissors

Whiteboard tools

- Pen tray
- Select tool
- Delete button

Getting Started

Ask children what they know about the story of Goldilocks. Write their ideas on page 2 of the "Goldilocks's Story" Notebook file. Ensure that children remember the key elements of the story.

Mini-Lesson

1. Read the story on pages 3 to 6 of the Notebook file. Discuss who the story is about, where she goes, what she eats, what she sits on, and where she goes to sleep.

2. Challenge children to think of a different character and retell the story using the new character's name.

3. Repeat this activity in a similar way, choosing another element to substitute, such as the location or the food tried and so on.

4. Now explain to children that you would like them to help you create a new story that will be different but will follow the same pattern as the story of Goldilocks.

5. Display page 7 of the Notebook file. Explain that children will need to select one of the characters who will then replace Goldilocks in the story.

6. When they have chosen which character to use, invite a volunteer to press on the relevant image on the Notebook page.

7. Proceed through the story, reading aloud the text to children. On each page, ask them to make their selection, deleting the unwanted pictures and text.

8. When the story is complete, reread it with children, print it out, and make this available for children.

Independent Work

Set up an art area. Hand out copies of "Make Your Own Story" (p. 61) and ask children to cut out chosen pictures and stick them onto a larger sheet of paper to create a storyboard. Provide some extra sheets of paper with blank boxes for children to use for their own ideas for a character, a house, some items, and so on. Suggest that children write captions for their storyboard using emergent writing. Support younger or less-confident learners by scribing their ideas, if necessary.

Wrap-Up

Use the Notebook file to remind children of the story of Goldilocks. Encourage the different groups to share with one another the Notebook files they have created.

Word Circle Game

Learning objectives
- To hear and say sounds in words in the order in which they occur.
- To link sounds to letters, naming and sounding the letters of the alphabet.

Resources
- "Word Circle Game" Notebook file
- "Circle Game" (p. 62)

Whiteboard tools
- Pen tray
- Select tool
- On-screen Keyboard

Getting Started

Open page 2 of the "Word Circle Game" Notebook file. Ask children to name and sound each letter. Demonstrate how the word *cat* can be made by using some of the letters at the bottom of the page. Press on the appropriate letters and drop them into the orange box. Use a Pen from the Pen tray or the On-screen Keyboard to write or type the word on the right-hand side of the page and then drag the letters in the orange box back to their original position at the bottom of the page.

Invite children to think of another word they could make using some of the letters. Suggest that they share this with their partner. Allow sufficient time for them to discuss their ideas and to agree on one. Invite a pair to come to the SMART Board and make the word in the orange box. Before they drag the letters back (ready for the next pair to take a turn), remind them to write the word on the right-hand side so that the group can remember which words have been created. Repeat until all possible words have been created.

Mini-Lesson, Part 1

1. Divide the class into groups of six.

2. Copy "Circle Game" (p. 62) onto cardstock and cut out the individual letters.

3. Display page 3 of the Notebook file and hand out the corresponding letters (one letter per child). Tell children that the first word is *fat*. Point to the word and ask children to check that the word is correct by saying the individual letter sounds and then the whole word.

4. Now challenge children to make the word *pat* in their heads, by changing one of the letters in the word *fat*. Ask what letter they took away and which letter they added to change the word.

5. Invite children to look at the letter they are holding. Is it the one needed to make the word *pat*? Ask the child holding the letter *p* to come to the SMART Board to change the word in the red box.

6. Ask everyone to check that the word is correct by sounding out the word together. Ask the child at the board to write the new word under the word *fat* on the right-hand side of the page.

7. Explain to children that their challenge is to keep making new words by changing only one letter sound at a time. They must try to think of all the words they can using the letters on the Notebook page, and get back to the word *fat* at the end.

8. Repeat the process with the group, so that children create the words in the sequence: *fat, pat, cat, can, pan, fan, fat.*

9. Make sure that each child has the opportunity to use the tools on the SMART Board. Support younger or less-confident learners by writing out the new words for them, if necessary.

(continued)

Mini-Lesson, Part 2

1. Repeat the activity in the next session, using pages 4 to 11 as appropriate with your groups. Explain to children that the letter pairs *ck* and *ee* have single sounds that can be replaced or added as though they are one letter. The following word lists can be created from the pages:

   - Page 4: *shop, ship, tip, tap, tack, back, bat, cat, cap, cop, shop*
   - Page 5: *song, sing, ring, rung, sung, sang, bang, back, sack, sick, sock, song*
   - Page 6: *slip, clip, flip, flap, slap, slack, black, flack, flick, slick, slip*
   - Page 7: *best, belt, bent, pent, pelt, melt, met, net, nest, best*
   - Page 8: *list, lift, gift, sift, silt, silk, sink, rink, rick, lick, lip, lisp, list*
   - Page 9: *teen, tin, sin, seen, seep, steep, sleep, slip, tip, tin, teen*
   - Page 10: *born, corn, cord, ford, fort, port, pork, fork, cork, stork, storm, torn, born*
   - Page 11: *mice, mine, line, life, wife, wine, wipe, wide, hide, hike, mike, mice*

2. Display an appropriate page for children to work on. Help them to generate their own word list by changing one letter (or letter sound) at a time as you did together in the previous lesson.

3. Explain that at the end of the session children will be able to share their work with the rest of the class. Ensure that you save their work in a separate file.

Independent Work

Provide appropriate letter collections and have these available in your writing center so that children can practice making words of their own.

Wrap-Up

Open Notebook pages that children have worked on to create their own lists and celebrate their work. Read down the lists, discussing which letter they have changed to make each new word. Talk together about the difference between words that begin with the same letter and words that rhyme together. Ask: *Do words that rhyme have to start with the same letter sound? Which bit of the word needs to sound the same for it to rhyme with another?* Use page 12 of the Notebook file to record children's comments.

Rhyming Game

Learning objectives
- To continue a rhyming string.
- To use their phonic knowledge to write simple regular words.

Resources
- "Rhyming Game" Notebook file
- individual whiteboards and pens
- a tray of objects

Whiteboard tools
- Pen tray
- Select tool
- Screen Shade
- Undo button

Getting Started

Display page 2 of the "Rhyming Game" Notebook file and ask children to say the sounds of the letters (*r*, *c*, *m*, *b*, *h*) as you point to them.

Next, say a letter sound and invite a child to come and point to it on the SMART Board page. Let that child say another letter sound, without pointing to it, and ask another child to come up and point to that letter.

Now invite children, in pairs, to blend the two letters *a* and *t* to find the rime. Invite one pair to tell you what it is. Ask the class to check this by sounding the individual letters and blending them.

Mini-Lesson, Part 1

1. Go to page 3 of the Notebook file. Ensure that children are sure what each picture represents. Point to one picture at a time and invite children to name the object (*rat*, *cat*, *bat*, *hat*, *mat*).

2. Demonstrate how you can move the individual letters and the -*at* rime together to create words. Choose one of the objects on the page and move it next to the rime. Select the appropriate letter (the onset) to make the word. Ask children to say the word with you. Ask: *Is this the correct word to match this picture?*

3. Next, make a deliberate mistake and create a word that does not match the picture. Ask children to tell you what you need to do to make the correct word.

4. Press the Undo button until the page is reset and invite a volunteer to try making a word to match one of the pictures on the SMART Board. Say the word together and check that it matches the picture.

5. Continue in this way until all the pictures have been named.

6. Say all the words in a list as you point to each picture. What do children notice about the words? (They rhyme and they use the same spelling pattern.) Listen to children's explanations and ideas and jot down notes about any children who show particularly good understanding or who will need some extra help.

7. Ask children if they can think of any more words that belong to this family of words. Write down any further suggestions on the SMART Board page. Look carefully at the spelling patterns of the words that children have suggested. Are they the same?

8. Go to page 4 of the Notebook file. Explain to children that you would like them to try to make some more words that rhyme with *at*. Invite them to tell you how they think they could do this. Show them an example, by dragging the rime (-*at*) and dropping it after one of the letters (the onset). Ask: *What word have I made?*

9. Provide children with individual whiteboards and pens and ask them to try making some words using the letters and rime displayed on the SMART Board.

10. Share some of children's ideas and invite individuals to come to the board to demonstrate how they made one of their words. Ensure that children realize that *gat* isn't a real word.

11. Go to page 5. Remind children of the words that rhyme with *at* that they have already made. Invite a child to explain how he or she made those words.

(continued)

12. Explain that you would like children to use their individual whiteboards to write down the words that they can make using the available letters.

13. Repeat the activity using page 6 of the Notebook file. Explain that you would like children to make as many -*at* words as possible.

Mini-Lesson, Part 2

1. Display page 7 of the Notebook file. Read the words underneath each picture. Encourage children to read them rhythmically with you: *hat, cat, mat, bat, rat.* Chant this with children a few times.

2. Explain to children that you are now going to hide the objects with the Screen Shade. Tell them that when it goes up, one of the objects will be missing! They must think hard to try and figure out which object is missing.

3. Remind children of the objects by repeating the chant.

4. Go to page 8 and pull the Screen Shade down slowly from the top. Ask: *What object is missing?* Repeat the chant to help children work out the answer.

5. Go back to page 7, look at the objects, then go to page 9. Pull the screen down slowly to display the objects on the page. Again, use the chant to help children figure out which object is missing.

6. Repeat the game on pages 10, 11, and 12.

7. Suggest that pairs of older or more-confident learners play the same game using pages 13 to 18 and 19 to 24 of the Notebook file.

Independent Work

Play a variation of the Rhyming Game using real objects. If possible, find five objects that rhyme and place them on a tray. Talk with children about the objects. Ask them to close their eyes while you remove one object. Talk about the objects and see if children can figure out which object is missing. Once they have figured it out, replace the object. Repeat, removing a different object each time.

Leave the tray of objects available to play the Rhyming Game. Encourage children to gather their own group of five objects they can use when they play the game.

Wrap-Up

Go to page 25 of the Notebook file. Remind children how they can select an initial sound and a rime to make words. Repeat the activity that children completed earlier in the lesson (making -*at* words), but this time they are going to make words with the rime -*an*.

If appropriate, use page 26 (featuring the rime -*ed*) with children. Be prepared to discuss the spellings of words such as *head* and *said*, which rhyme, but are spelled differently.

Making Words

Learning objective
- To hear and say sounds in words in the order in which they occur.

Resources
- "Making Words" Notebook file
- "Make Words" (p. 63)

Whiteboard tools
- Pen tray
- Select tool

Getting Started

Provide each child with a copy of the reproducible "Make Words" (p. 63). Help children cut out the letter cards on the right-hand side of the page so that each child has a set of six letter cards.

Pair up children and explain that you would like them to put the letters in the word frame to spell different words. Tell them that the first word is *cat*. Ask children to talk to their partner and decide what initial sound is needed to make the word *cat*. Invite one of the children to tell you what sound this is and then ask the class whether this is correct. Once everyone is agreed on the letter, ask children to place the correct letter card in the initial position on the word frame on their reproducible sheets.

Now ask children to discuss with their partner the next sound in the word. Again, they should place this letter card in the correct position on the word frame. Finally, ask them to discuss the ending sound in the word and place the letter card in the final position on the word frame.

Mini-Lesson

1. Display page 2 of the "Making Words" Notebook file. Explain to children that they need to make the word *rat* using the available letters. Show them that by pressing on each letter they can listen to the sound it makes and by pressing on the picture they can listen to the word they are supposed to make.

2. Encourage children to talk to their partner and decide what is the initial sound needed to make the word *rat*. Invite a volunteer to tell you what sound this is and ask him or her to press on a letter to find the sound.

3. Invite the child to press on the colored strip at the foot of the letter and move it to the initial position in the word frame.

4. Repeat for the remaining letters.

5. Practice this procedure to make other words on pages 3 to 10 of the Notebook file.

6. Go to page 11. Explain that children need to make the word *sun* using the letters, but that this time there are too many letters. Help them to do this and continue to support them as they work through pages 11 to 16.

Independent Work

Repeat the activity from Getting Started, encouraging children to use different words.

Wrap-Up

Go to page 17 of the Notebook file. Check that the word *dog* has been made correctly in the word frame. Explain that the remaining letters may also be arranged to make a word. Ask children to say each sound and invite them to help you arrange the letters to make the word *dog*. Ask: *What word can we make with the remaining letters?* Move the remaining letters together in a row. Ask children to discuss with their partner whether this makes a word. Select one of the pairs to tell the rest of the group their decision. Ask another child to rearrange the letters to make a word. What does the word say? Say it together. Repeat this activity on pages 18 and 19.

Robotic Words

Learning objective

- To read a range of familiar and common words independently.

Resources

- "Robotic Words" Notebook file
- paper and colored markers
- a variety of objects or toys that fit the CVC pattern spelling, such as a dog, a cat, a mug, and a can

Whiteboard tools

- Pen tray
- Select tool
- Lines tool

Getting Started

Show the objects that fit the CVC (consonant–vowel–consonant) spelling pattern to children, one at a time. Make sure children know what they all are.

Display page 2 of the "Robotic Words" Notebook file. Ask children what the picture shows (a robot). Invite a volunteer to speak how they think a robot might speak. Listen to various suggestions and then explain carefully how this robot speaks (by saying the sound of each letter individually). Demonstrate by pointing to one of the objects that you have just shown children, saying each letter individually. For example: *m–u–g*.

Explain to children that you are now going to write the name of one of the objects in the speech bubble. Do this using a Pen from the Pen tray and read it robotically. Ask children to repeat this and then to blend the sounds to make the word.

Use the Eraser from the Pen tray to erase the word in the speech bubble, then write the name of another object and repeat. Ask children to sound out each letter and then to say the word with you.

Group Activity

1. Display page 3 of the Notebook file. Press on the first word and listen to the robot speak.

2. Remind children of how the robot speaks and suggest that they can use the sounds that the robot makes to work out what each word is and then match it to the correct picture.

3. Make sure that children know what each picture represents and show them that if they are unsure of what a picture is they may press on it to hear the word.

4. Support children, as necessary, to move the words to match the pictures on page 3. Show them how to use the Lines tool to add arrows to link the words to the pictures.

5. Put children in pairs or small groups. Allow them to take turns working through pages 4 to 11 of the Notebook file.

Independent Work

Provide paper and colored markers for children to draw their own robots. Suggest that they make up a voice for their robot, where the robot says one letter at a time. Encourage children to work with a partner and use real objects, sounding out each letter separately as they spell each word. Ask them to invite their partner to guess the word they have made.

Wrap-Up

Review the work that children did, using the pages of the Notebook file. Make sure that everyone understands how to sound out the robot's letter sounds and can match the words to the pictures accurately.

Words That Rhyme

Learning objective

- To practice and become confident in making rhymes.

Resources

- "Words That Rhyme" Notebook file
- "Rhyming Words" (p. 64), one copy for each child, cut up and mounted onto cardstock and laminated with punched-out holes next to each word
- shoelaces or yarn to thread through the cards
- writing notebooks and pencils

Whiteboard tools

- Pen tray
- Highlighter pen
- Select tool

Getting Started

Open page 2 of the "Words That Rhyme" Notebook file. Explain that you are going to say two words, and ask children to identify whether the words rhyme or not (for example *cat* and *mat*, or *cat* and *can*). Have children show a "thumbs-up" sign if the words rhyme and a "thumbs-down" sign if they don't. Ask children for other examples of words that rhyme and assess their responses. Give the opportunity for a more-confident learner to explain what *rhyme* means.

Mini-Lesson

1. Go to page 3 of the Notebook file and ask a more-confident reader to read the first sentence clearly to the class.

2. Encourage children to find the rhyming words within the sentence and share them with a talking partner.

3. Select one pair of children to use a Highlighter pen to highlight the rhyming words. Ask the rest of the class: *Have they highlighted the correct words?*

4. Point out that words that rhyme sound the same at the end and often have the same spelling of the word ending.

5. Repeat this process for the other two sentences.

6. Go to page 4 and ask what word goes with the picture. Move the magnifying glass beneath the picture to check.

7. Read the words on the right-hand side with children. Explain that one of the words on the right-hand side rhymes with *cat*. Ask children to discuss with their talking partners which word they think it is. When pressed, the correct word will "cheer."

8. Repeat this for pages 5 to 12.

Independent Work

Give out the "Rhyming Words" cards you have prepared (p. 64) and ask children to read all of the words carefully. Demonstrate how to thread a shoelace through the holes to join rhyming words. When children have completed the threading, encourage them to compare their answers with a partner and discuss any differences. Ask children to write the pairs of rhyming words in their notebooks, looking carefully at their spelling.

Limit the number of words for less-confident learners. As an extension challenge, ask children to think of another word that rhymes with the two they have already found.

Wrap-Up

Go to page 13 of the Notebook file. Make the word *cat* on the first line by dragging the *c* next to the *-at* rime and ask a child to read the word. Challenge children to think of words that rhyme with *cat*. When a child thinks of a real word, allow them to drag the correct letter from the box and add it to one of the *-at* rimes to make the word. Read all of the words together and establish that they do rhyme.

CVC Words, Part 1

Learning objective
- To segment words into their constituent phonemes in order to spell them correctly.

Resources
- "CVC Words, Part 1" Notebook file
- "CVC Words" (p. 65)
- a letter fan for each child containing every letter of the alphabet (see Before You Start)

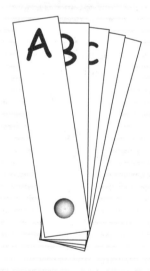

Whiteboard tools
- Pen tray
- Select tool

Before You Start

To make a letter fan, take thirteen 3" x 5" index cards and cut them in half lengthwise. Write a letter of the alphabet near the top of each card. Punch a hole near the bottom of the cards. Put the cards in alphabetical order, then fasten them together with a brass fastener.

Getting Started

Open page 2 of the "CVC Words, Part 1" Notebook file. Give each child or pair a letter fan and explain how to use it. Say a letter sound and have children locate and show the letter. Assess their level of understanding of sound-letter correspondence. Move on to ask them to show initial, final, and medial sounds in CVC words as appropriate.

Mini-Lesson

1. Go to page 3 of the Notebook file and introduce the two characters, Billy and Kelly the Kind Fairy.

2. Using pages 4 to 9, help the fairy change *man* into *pet* by changing one letter in the word at a time.

3. When the word is first displayed, say each letter sound separately then blend them together and say the whole word. Ask a child to identify the new word to be made from the picture clue on the right-hand side of the page.

4. Encourage children to choose which letter they need to change and what it should be changed to.

5. Invite a volunteer to come to the SMART Board, select the correct letter, and drag and drop it into the appropriate position in the word.

6. Once the new word is made, say each letter sound separately, then blend them together and say the whole word. Ask: *Have we made the correct word?*

7. Next, show the CVC words on pages 10 to 17 one at a time. Ask children to work out what letter is missing from each of the words and show the answer using their letter fans.

8. Invite a child to drag the correct letter into place on the SMART Board.

Independent Work

Give out copies of "CVC Words" (p. 65). Ensure that everyone knows what each picture shows. Tell children that they must fill in the missing letter for each CVC word. Encourage them to say the word slowly and then segment it into the three letter sounds. Display an alphabet to support forming letters correctly.

To help develop the ability of less-confident learners to hear initial and final sounds, give them a set of pictures or objects to sort by initial or final sounds.

Wrap-Up

Go to page 18 of the Notebook file. Ask a child to segment the word into three letters by dragging them apart. Ask another child to say the three letter sounds separately. Drag the three letters back together again to recreate the whole word and demonstrate how to blend the letter sounds by saying them more quickly in order to read the word. Repeat this with pages 19 to 21, but ask children to blend the letter sounds and tell a partner what the word is before sharing the answer with the class.

CVC Words, Part 2

Learning objective

- To apply phonic knowledge as the prime approach to reading and spelling unfamiliar words that are not completely decodable.

Resources

- "CVC Words, Part 2" Notebook file
- letter fan for each child containing every letter of the alphabet (see Before You Start, p. 26)
- three six-sided CVC dice for each group, labeled as follows: *b, t, s, n, m, p; a, e, i, i, o, u; g, p, t, s, n, d*
- individual whiteboards and pens
- paper and pencils

Whiteboard tools

- Pen tray
- On-screen Keyboard
- Select tool

Getting Started

Display page 2 of the "CVC Words, Part 2" Notebook file. Discuss the different strategies that can be used for decoding an unfamiliar word. Focus on the suggestion that a word can be sounded out. Ask children to explain what this means and how they would do it.

Go to page 3 and ask children to read the sentences aloud. Discuss how they tackled any unfamiliar words.

Mini-Lesson

1. Go to page 4 of the Notebook file and explain that children are going to find out how many real words they can make using the letter cards.

2. Demonstrate how to say the separate letter sounds in the word *tug* and then blend them together to read the whole word. Ask: *Is it a real word?* Clarify any misconceptions.

3. Drag the *t* card into the bin and then ask children to blend the next three phonemes displayed (*f–u–g*). Again, ask children to decide whether the word is real or not.

4. Next drag the *u* card into the bin and repeat the blending. Then drag the *g* card into the bin. Continue to remove cards in order (left to right) until you get to *pat*.

5. Encourage children to list real words on the page at the side of the bin.

6. Provide children with individual whiteboards and pens. Ask them to read the CVC words on page 5 and then choose three words that they think are real and write them on their boards.

7. Discuss as a class and ask a volunteer to sort the words by dragging them into the correct columns on the Notebook page.

Independent Work

Give each similar-ability group a set of three CVC dice (see Resources) and tell them to roll each one. They then put the dice into CVC order (dice may need to be color-coded to support this). As a group, children blend the letter sounds and decide if they make a real word. They should list the real words on paper.

Blend the VC rime for less-confident learners, asking them only to add the initial consonant. Challenge more-confident learners by altering one of the consonant dice to show initial consonant blends, so they can blend CCVC words.

Wrap-Up

Go to page 6 of the Notebook file. Press on "Word 1" to hear the word spoken aloud (*box*). Ask children to spell the word by dragging the correct letters up to the line. Check that the spelling is correct using the magnifying glass. Repeat with the second word.

Give each child a letter fan. Say a CVC word to children and ask them to make it with their letter fan. Ask one child with the correct answer on their fan to write the CVC word on the board. Assess which children need more support with spelling CVC words. Use page 7 to assess children's understanding of CVC words.

Color Words

Learning objective
- To recognize automatically an increasing number of familiar high-frequency words.

Resources
- "Color Words" Notebook file
- "Color Mixing" (p. 66)
- colored pens or pencils
- color pair cards (see Before You Start)
- ready-mix paint

Whiteboard tools
- Eraser
- Pen tray
- Highlighter pen
- Select tool

Before You Start
Make sets of six cards for each child, each card showing two colors that can be mixed into a third color (for example, red and yellow, yellow and blue, red and blue, and so on).

Getting Started
Ask children to think of as many different colors as they can. Go to page 2 of the "Color Words" Notebook file. Invite children to point out any color words that they recognize. Read the chant to them. Invite them to join in with the color words. Explain that the color of the words gives a clue as to what the color word says. Identify and highlight the rhymes in the chant.

Mini-Lesson
1. Go to page 3 of the Notebook file and ask children to name the colors in turn. Allow a child to wipe off the paint with the Eraser from the Pen tray as the color is named to reveal the color word underneath.

2. Examine the color words. Look at initial sounds and the shapes and spelling patterns within the words.

3. Go to page 4 and ask the class to read the color words and match them to the blobs of color.

4. Pages 5 to 8 extend children's understanding of color mixing as well as their color word knowledge.

5. Show page 5, read the color equation, and ask children what the answer is. Demonstrate with ready-mix paint if children are unsure.

6. Drag the correct color into place and read the whole equation. Then ask children to drag the correct labels onto each color.

7. Repeat for pages 6 to 8.

Independent Work
Give out copies of "Color Mixing" (p. 66) and the sets of prepared cards (see Before You Start). Children should pick a card and name the colors. Demonstrate how to color the first two blobs in the color sentence on their sheet to match the card. Ask children to decide which new color the two colors will make when they are mixed together and color the third blob that color. Encourage them to use the word bank at the top of the sheet to label the colors.

Work with the less-confident learners on pages 9 and 10 of the Notebook file to sort pictures of objects by their color. Extend this by sorting real objects, adding the correct color label to each group from a choice of three labels.

Wrap-Up
Take children into the hall and stick different color words on the walls with suitable gaps in between. Ask children to move around the hall in a variety of ways. When you say a color word they must find it on the wall and sit down in front of it. Assess which children need more support in reading color words.

Reading High-Frequency Words

Learning objective

- To recognize automatically an increasing number of familiar high-frequency words.

Resources

- "Reading High-Frequency Words" Notebook file
- counters (20 per pair)
- bingo boards and word cards (see Before You Start)

Whiteboard tools

- Pen tray
- Screen Shade
- Spotlight tool
- Select tool

Before You Start

Prepare a bingo board for each pair of children: a 5 x 4 grid with 20 high-frequency words in different places. Prepare individual cards of the same words.

Getting Started

Display page 2 of the "Reading High-Frequency Words" Notebook file and read the words with children. Focus on the shape of the word and point out any tall letters. Explain that looking at the shape of a word can help you recognize it. Challenge children to match the word shapes to the words. Drag the shapes over the words to check their ideas. Enable the Screen Shade to show only the shapes and not the words. Challenge children to recall which words belonged in each shape.

Mini-Lesson

1. Together, read the sentences on page 3 of the Notebook file and discuss the strategies used to work out any unfamiliar words.

2. Explain that the same sentences are written on the next pages but with a word missing. The correct spelling of the missing word must be chosen from a choice of four.

3. Work through pages 4 to 7 and discuss which of the words are spelled correctly. Use the Eraser from the Pen tray to rub over the blank space in the sentence to reveal the correct spelling of the word.

4. Use page 8 to assess children who have not yet contributed to the lesson. Ask a child to drag the first brick from the bottom right corner of the page and place it next to the word *here* to start building a wall.

5. Ask the same child to read the word. Allow children to ask for help if they are unsure. Continue this with different children until all the bricks have been used.

Independent Work

Give each pair of children a bingo board and 20 counters (see Before You Start). Read a word card to the class. Tell pairs to cover the word with a counter if it is on their board. Explain that they need to get a line of counters across the board to win the game, and that when they have done this they should call "bingo." Keep the called cards to one side so you can check the words that have been covered up on the winning team's card.

Less-confident learners will need to play this game in a small group with an adult supporting them. Encourage more-confident learners to work in their own groups, with one child designated as the caller.

Wrap-Up

Enable the Spotlight tool. Go to page 9 of the Notebook file and ask children to use the spotlight to find the words hidden in the ocean (change the words if necessary to match the needs of children). When they find a word, ask them to read it aloud. When they have found all of the words, ask a child to use the spotlight again to find a specific word.

Initial Consonant Blends, Part 1

Learning objective
- To recognize the spelling/sound correspondence of common consonant blends.

Resources
- "Initial Consonant Blends, Part 1" Notebook file
- "Is That a Word?" (p. 67)
- scissors and glue
- notebooks and pencils
- a fan for each child made of seven narrow cards, each showing a consonant blend (*br, cr, dr, fr, gr, pr, tr*), and fastened together with a brass fastener (see Before You Start, p. 26)

Whiteboard tools
- Eraser
- Pen tray
- Select tool
- Highlighter pen

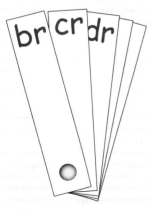

Getting Started
Open page 2 of the "Initial Consonant Blends, Part 1" Notebook file. Demonstrate how to blend the two letters *b* and *r* together to make the /br/ sound. Press the button to listen to the blend being spoken. Tell children that these two letters together are called a *consonant blend*.

Repeat the activity on pages 3 to 8. Encourage children to think of words beginning with the same consonant blend. Use the pictures on each page to get them started with this.

Mini-Lesson
1. Give each child a consonant blend fan (see Resources) and explain how to use it to show a consonant blend. Ask them to show specific sounds to ensure their knowledge of how to spell the sounds is secure.

2. Go to page 9 of the Notebook file and ask children to say what the picture shows. Repeat the word clearly.

3. Encourage them to decide for themselves which consonant blend the word begins with and to hold up that sound on their fan.

4. Assess children's answers, then ask one child to press the correct blend from the board. A cheer will be heard when the correct answer is pressed. Show the initial consonant blend by using the Eraser from the Pen tray to reveal the missing letters.

5. Blend the whole word together to check the answer. For example, *br–i–ck*, *brick*.

6. Repeat this activity on pages 10 to 18.

Independent Work
Provide each child with a copy of "Is That a Word?" (p. 67). Ask children to cut out each word individually. Invite them to read each word by blending the sounds together. Tell them to sort the words into two piles as they read them—"real words" and "not real words." They should then stick the real words into their notebooks. Below each word, encourage children to write a simple sentence containing the word.

Give less-confident learners the real words only, to sort by their initial consonant blend to aid discrimination skills. After sorting the words, support children in blending the sounds to read them. Challenge more-confident learners by asking them to think of their own words that begin with a given consonant blend.

Wrap-Up
Work through the words on the sheet and identify whether each word is a real word or not. Encourage children to assess their own success in this task. Go to page 19 of the Notebook file. Press on the top word (*brid*) and ask children if it is a real word or not. Following their decision, invite a volunteer to drag and drop the word into the correct column on the page. Repeat the activity for the rest of the words on the page. Ask individual children to blend the words and sort them, assessing the learning that has taken place in the lesson.

Initial Consonant Blends, Part 2

Learning objective

- To recognize the spelling/sound correspondence of common consonant blends.

Resources

- "Initial Consonant Blends, Part 2" Notebook file
- "Pairing Socks" (p. 68). Before the lesson, make one enlarged copy, cut out the socks, and laminate them.
- a fan for each child made of six narrow cards, each showing a consonant blend (*bl, cl, fl, gl, pl, sl*), and fastened together with a brass fastener (see Before You Start, p. 26)
- notebooks and pencils

Whiteboard tools

- Pen tray
- Select tool
- Delete button

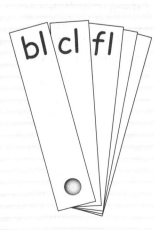

Getting Started

Open page 2 of the "Initial Consonant Blends, Part 2" Notebook file. Demonstrate how to blend the two letters *s* and *l* together to make the /sl/ sound. Press the button to listen to the blend being spoken. Tell children that these two letters together are called a *consonant blend*.

Repeat the activity on pages 3 to 7. Encourage children to think of words beginning with the same consonant blend. Use the pictures on each page to get them started with this.

Mini-Lesson

1. Give each child a consonant blend fan (see Resources) and explain how to use it to show a consonant blend. Ask them to show specific sounds to ensure their knowledge of how to spell the sounds is secure.

2. Display page 8 of the Notebook file. Ask children to identify what the picture shows. Repeat the word clearly.

3. Encourage them to decide for themselves which consonant blend the word begins with and to hold up that sound on their fans.

4. Assess children's answers, then invite one child to drag two letters from the bottom of the page onto the line at the beginning of the word to make the correct blend. Use the Delete button to delete the box concealing the word to check the answer.

5. Finally, blend the whole word together to check the answer. For example, *sl–u–g, slug*.

6. Repeat this activity on pages 9 to 13.

Independent Work

Give out copies of "Pairing Socks" (p. 68). Explain to children that they must make pairs of socks by matching a consonant blend onset to a rime to make a real word. Invite them to write the words they make in their notebooks. Below each word, encourage them to write a simple sentence containing the word.

Less-confident learners could match socks that have been cut out and laminated. The socks could be color-coded to aid the matching process. After making the words, help children blend the onset and rime to read them. Challenge more-confident learners by asking them to think of different ways of pairing the socks (for example, *clip, clan, blob, blot*) and to make their own words that begin with a given consonant blend.

Wrap-Up

Use the enlarged and laminated socks to share the answers to the work done on the sheet. Ask children to choose two socks that make a word and hold them up together. Encourage them to assess their own success in this task. Display page 14 of the Notebook file. Read the onsets and rimes on the page. Ask individual children to match the onsets to the rimes to make a real word. Assess the learning that has taken place in the lesson.

Ending Consonant Blends

Learning objective
• To recognize the spelling/sound correspondence of common consonant blends.

Resources
• "Ending Consonant Blends" Notebook file
• "Bingo Blends" (p. 69), enlarged to 11" x 17" and cut into boards and individual cards
• counters
• for each child, a fan made of six narrow cards, each showing a conso-nant blend (*st*, *sp*, *sk*, *nd*, *nt*, *nk*), and fastened together with a brass fastener (see Before You Start, p. 26)

Whiteboard tools
• Pen tray
• Select tool
• Highlighter pen

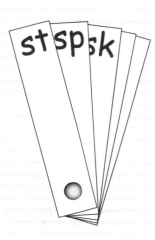

Getting Started
Open page 2 of the "Ending Consonant Blends" Notebook file. Demonstrate how to blend the two letters *s* and *t* together to make the /st/ sound. Ask children to blend the sounds together on pages 3 to 7. Press the button on each page to listen to the blend being spoken. Tell children that these two letters together are called *consonant blends*. Explain that consonant blends can be at the end of a word as well as at the beginning of it. Ask them to think of words ending with each of the blends.

Mini-Lesson
1. Give each child a consonant blend fan (see Resources) and explain how to use it to show a consonant blend. Ask children to show specific sounds to ensure their knowledge of how to spell the sounds is secure.

2. Look at page 8 of the Notebook file and read the words at the bottom of the page together.

3. Ask a child to choose one of the words and read it aloud. Invite the rest of the class to show which consonant blend the word ends with by holding up the appropriate blend on their fans.

4. Sort all of the words by dragging and dropping them into the correct group on the Notebook page.

5. Repeat this activity on page 9.

Independent Work
Put children into similar-ability groups of three. Give each group two bingo boards and a set of word cards created from "Bingo Blends" (p. 69), plus some counters. Go to page 10 of the Notebook file and explain the rules of the game to children. Ensure the caller checks the other players' choices and corrects them if necessary.

Support less-confident learners with reading the word cards and show the cards to the players to help them find the correct final blend if necessary. Encourage more-confident learners to think of other words ending in these consonant blends.

Wrap-Up
Go to page 11 of the Notebook file. Ask children to read the words on the cards at the bottom of the page and highlight the consonant blends in each of them. Tell children that these words are answers to the clues above. Ask them to read out each clue and then work as a class to match the answer cards to them. Invite volunteers to drag and drop the words into the appropriate spaces next to the clues. Repeat this activity on page 12.

Spelling High-Frequency Words

Learning objective
- To learn to spell some common irregular words.

Resources
- "Spelling High-Frequency Words" Notebook file
- individual whiteboards and pens
- sheet of paper with five spelling words (see Before You Start)
- strips of cardboard

Whiteboard tools
- Pen tray
- Select tool
- On-screen Keyboard
- Screen Shade

Before You Start
Each child needs a "look–cover–write–check" sheet suitable for their level of ability: list five words down the side of a sheet of paper, then add three more short lines after each word across the page (see page 3 of the Notebook file for reference). Also provide strips of cardboard to cover words on the sheet.

Getting Started
Display page 2 of the "Spelling High-Frequency Words" Notebook file. Explain that the groups of letters are anagrams of color words and that the color of the letters gives a clue to what the words should say. Challenge children to reorder the letters so that each color word is spelled correctly.

Mini-Lesson
1. Go to page 3 of the Notebook file. If you need to change the words so that they are appropriate for the needs of your children, double-click on the word and use the On-screen Keyboard to type in a different word.

2. Provide children with individual whiteboards and pens.

3. Explain the process of learning spellings using the look–cover–write–check method: Tell children to look closely at the first word and think about its shape, length, and any familiar letter patterns. Move the cover over the word and ask children to write it on their individual whiteboards. Invite a volunteer to write the word in the white box on the Notebook page. Uncover the word and encourage children to check their spelling against it.

4. Repeat for the other four words on the page.

5. Try the word-tracking activities on pages 4 to 8 to help children focus on the letter order in each of the words. (Change the words and letters to match the words used on page 3 if you have altered these already.)

6. Ask a child to track along the row of letters from left to right and drag the correct letters into the box at the bottom of the page as they reach them to build the word.

Independent Work
Give each child a prepared sheet of words and a strip of cardboard (see Before You Start). Explain that children have ten minutes to look at each word carefully, cover it up with the strip of card, write it, and then check it. Tell them not to look at the words while they write them. They should practice each word three times using the lines provided. Stress that look–cover–write–check is a good strategy for learning new spellings. The words used should be differentiated for less-confident and more-confident learners.

Wrap-Up
Use page 9 of the Notebook file to give children a spelling test. Ask them to spell the five words that they learned on page 3. Use the Screen Shade to hide the words. Then invite children to swap their work with a friend and check against the board. Once they have completed this, test each group on the spelling of the five words they learned during their independent work.

Missing Words

Learning objective
- To use syntax and context when reading for meaning.

Resources
- "Missing Words" Notebook file
- picture book with a few words covered with sticky notes
- individual whiteboards and pens
- index cards
- notebooks and pencils

Whiteboard tools
- Eraser
- Pen tray
- Select tool

Before You Start

Before the lesson, write simple sentences with a word missing from them onto individual cards. For example, *We read _____ book in class. I like to _____ orange juice. After school, it's time ____ go home.*

Getting Started

With children, discuss different strategies they can use to decode unfamiliar words. Remind them particularly of using the text in the rest of the sentence to figure out a word. Explain that it is often helpful to reread the sentence or read the rest of the sentence and then go back and try to fill in the missing word.

Read the picture book (see Resources) and use the strategies discussed to guess what the covered words might be.

Mini-Lesson

1. Open page 2 of the "Missing Words" Notebook file. Tell children that some words are missing from the sentences. You would like them to figure out the missing words.

2. Ask them to explain how they could figure out each missing word. Refer them back to the strategies discussed in Getting Started.

3. Invite a child to read the first sentence, leaving a blank for the missing word.

4. Provide each pair of children with an individual whiteboard and a pen. Ask them to write down their idea of what the missing word is.

5. Listen to some of children's ideas and try them in the sentence. Discuss which words work, and which do not.

6. Use the Eraser from the Pen tray to rub over the empty spaces in each sentence to reveal what the missing word actually is.

7. Repeat this for all of the sentences on pages 2 and 3 of the Notebook file.

Independent Work

Divide the class into small groups and give a set of prepared sentence cards to each group (see Before You Start). Tell children to read the sentences on the cards and discuss what the missing words could be with a talking partner in their group. Suggest they try the words in the sentences to see if they make sense. Ask them to write the sentences in their notebooks with the missing words included.

Support less-confident learners by giving them a choice of two words to put into the blank. Ask them to decide which of the two words makes sense in the sentence. Encourage more-confident learners to make up their own "missing word" sentences, to try on each other.

Wrap-Up

Go to page 4 of the Notebook file. Discuss some of the sentences children have investigated. Listen to some of the ideas that children had about what the missing words could be. Discuss which of the ideas would work and which would not, and explain why. Make notes on the board.

Long-e Vowel Sound

Learning objective
- To recognize/use alternative ways of spelling the phonemes already taught (e.g., long-e sound spelled as *ea* and *ee*).

Resources
- "Long-e Vowel Sound" Notebook file
- "*ee* or *ea*?" (p. 70)
- picture book that contains the long-e vowel sound
- individual whiteboards and pens

Whiteboard tools
- Pen tray
- Highlighter pen
- Select tool
- Delete button

Getting Started

Introduce the long-e vowel sound. Go to page 2 of the "Long-e Vowel Sound" Notebook file and show children two different ways of spelling the long-e sound (*ee* and *ea*). Demonstrate the sound it makes in words.

Read the picture book as a class. Ask children to indicate every time they hear a word containing the long-e sound. Write some of the words on page 2 and highlight the letters responsible for the sound.

Mini-Lesson

1. Go to page 3 of the Notebook file. Ask individual children to read the words on the page and point out that all of the words contain the long-e sound spelled using *ee*.

2. Now look at page 4, but this time point out that all of the words contain the long-e sound spelled using *ea*.

3. Challenge children to think of other words containing the long-e sound that were not on the two pages.

4. Read the sentences on page 5 and identify the words that contain the long-e sound. Ask individual children to highlight these words and identify which letters each contains.

5. Show children page 6 of the Notebook file. Ask them to name the picture, decide which spelling is correct, and to write it on their individual whiteboards.

6. After they have done this, use the Delete button (or select the Delete option from the drop-down menu) to remove the blue rectangle to check the answer.

7. Repeat this activity on pages 7 to 10, to identify children who need more support.

Independent Work

Provide each child with a copy of "*ee* or *ea*?" (p. 70). Discuss what each picture shows. Remind children that each word contains a long-e sound. Ask children to complete the spellings by adding the correct letters—*ee* or *ea*.

Show more-confident learners how to use a dictionary to check words that they are unsure how to spell. Encourage them to support the less-confident learners in finding the words. Then read the sentences together and ensure everyone knows what the words with the missing letters are. Ask children to fill in the missing letters in the sentences, encouraging them to check their spellings using a simple dictionary.

Wrap-Up

Encourage children to check their answers with a friend from a different table, discussing any answers that are different. Support children in resolving disagreements by showing them how to check the words in a simple dictionary. Show the class page 11 of the Notebook file and ask them to identify the sound that *ee* and *ea* make. Give out individual whiteboards and ask children to write down four words containing the long-e sound. List these on the board.

Long-o Vowel Sound

Learning objective
- To recognize/use alternative ways of spelling the phonemes already taught (e.g., long-o sound spelled as *oa* and *ow*).

Resources
- "Long-o Vowel Sound" Notebook file
- "*oa* or *ow*?" (p. 71)
- picture book that contains the long-o vowel sound
- individual whiteboards and pens

Whiteboard tools
- Pen tray
- Select tool
- Highlighter pen
- Fill Color tool
- Eraser

Getting Started

Go to page 2 of the "Long-o Vowel Sound" Notebook file. Introduce the long-o vowel sound. Show children two different ways of spelling the long-o sound (*oa* and *ow*). Demonstrate the sound it makes in words.

Read the picture book as a class. Ask children to indicate every time they hear a word containing the long-o sound. Write some of the words on page 2 and highlight the letters responsible for the sound in each word.

Mini-Lesson

1. Go to page 3 of the Notebook file and ask children to read the two sets of letters. Note that they make the same sound even though they are spelled differently.

2. Challenge children to think of words containing the long-o sound and write them on page 3.

3. Read the words on the cards on page 4 of the Notebook file. Encourage children to sort the words into the correct columns, then read each list together.

4. Ask a child to press the sound icons on page 5 and tell the class to listen carefully to the words.

5. Invite children to write on their individual whiteboards the words they hear, considering the spelling carefully. Check the words as a class.

6. Go to page 6 and ask children to decide, in pairs, which answer goes with which clue.

7. Drag the answers to the side of each clue and then use the Fill Color tool to change the red boxes to white to check them.

Independent Work

Give out copies of "*oa* or *ow*?" (p. 71) and put children into mixed-ability pairs. Ensure that all children understand how to complete a crossword. Encourage the more-confident learner in each pair to support the less able with filling in the answers correctly. Ask children to read the clues in their pairs and work out what the answers could be. Remind them regularly that the answers to the clues all contain the long-o sound. Tell children to fill in the words on their own crossword sheet, ensuring that they spell them correctly. Support children in using a dictionary to check any spellings of words that they are unsure about. As an extension, challenge children to think of other words containing the long-o sound.

Wrap-Up

Show children a correctly completed crossword. Ask them to check their own answers and assess their own success. Use page 7 of the Notebook file to assess any children whom you are still unsure about. Discuss any errors made and correct them. Finally, use the Eraser from the Pen tray to reveal the answers.

/oo/ Vowel Sound

Learning objective

- To recognize/use alternative ways of spelling the phonemes already taught (e.g., /oo/ sound spelled with *oo*, *ew*, and *ue*).

Resources

- "/oo/ Vowel Sound" Notebook file
- "*oo*, *ew*, or *ue*?" (p. 72)
- picture book that contains the /oo/ sound
- index cards

Whiteboard tools

- Pen tray
- Highlighter pen
- Select tool

Before You Start

Before the lesson, make a set of three cards for each child, each card displaying a different spelling for the /oo/ sound—*oo*, *ew*, *ue*.

Getting Started

Go to page 2 of the "/oo/ Vowel Sound" Notebook file. Introduce the vowel sound /oo/. Show children three different ways to spell the /oo/ sound (*oo*, *ew*, and *ue*). Demonstrate the sound it makes in words.

Read the picture book as a class. Ask children to indicate every time they hear a word containing the /oo/ sound. Write some of the words on the Notebook page, and highlight the letters in each word that is responsible for the sound.

Mini-Lesson

1. Go to page 3 of the Notebook file and read the words at the bottom of the page. Elicit from children that all of the words contain the /oo/ sound.

2. Challenge children to sort the words into the correct boxes according to the letters they contain.

3. Read the sentences on page 4 of the Notebook file and work out together what the words with missing letters should say.

4. Give out the set of three cards (see Before You Start) to each child and ask them to show the letters they think are missing from each word.

5. Decide as a class on the correct spelling and drag the letters into place.

6. Challenge children to think of other words that contain the /oo/ vowel sound.

7. Invite individual children to come to the SMART Board to write words containing the /oo/ sound on page 5. Ask other children to highlight the letters that make the /oo/ sound in the word written.

Independent Work

Hand out copies of "*oo*, *ew*, or *ue*?" (p. 72). Ask children to read the words in the word bank at the bottom of the sheet quietly to themselves. Support less-confident learners by clarifying any words they are unsure of. Read the sentences together and explain that each word in the word bank fits into one of the blanks in the sentences, so that the sentence makes sense. Encourage children to reread the sentences with the word fitted in, to check that they make sense.

Wrap-Up

Make three cards that clearly display each spelling for the /oo/ sound—*oo*, *ew*, *ue*. Stick the cards on different walls of the school hall or other large open space. Ask children to note where each card is. Tell them they must listen to the word you say and then select the letters it contains. Say a word and encourage children to move toward the card that has the letters the word contains. Repeat this with other words. Watch carefully for children who follow the crowd, as these may need more help with learning the vowel sound /oo/.

Silent *e*

Learning objective

- To recognize/use alternative ways of spelling the phonemes already taught (e.g., long-a sound spelled with *ai*, *ay*, or *a–e*).

Resources

- "Silent *e*" Notebook file
- "Add the *e*" (p. 73) copied on cardstock for each group of students and cut apart
- individual whiteboards and pens
- pencils

Whiteboard tools

- Eraser
- Pen tray
- Select tool
- Highlighter pen

Getting Started

Review the different ways to spell each of the long vowel sounds. Go to page 2 of the "Silent *e*" Notebook file and explain that these sounds can also be created with a silent *e*. Explain that this is made using a vowel, then a consonant or consonant blend, then an *e*. When the *e* is added, it tells the vowel to make a long sound instead of the short sound it would usually make. Write a few examples on the board to illustrate these points (for example, *mat* and *mate*, *rid* and *ride*, *tub* and *tube*).

Sing the song on page 3, to the tune of "This Old Man," to help children remember this new concept.

Mini-Lesson

1. Look at page 4 of the Notebook file and read the words. Point out that each vowel makes a short sound.

2. Challenge children to add a silent *e* to the end of each word on their individual whiteboards, and investigate how the words change.

3. Use the Eraser from the Pen tray to check the words created and read them aloud.

4. Emphasize the change the vowel has made, from a short sound to a long sound. Remind children this has happened because of the silent *e*.

5. Tell children to read and sort the words on the cards on page 5 using their silent *e* knowledge. Emphasize the long vowel sound created in each word.

6. Ask children to think of sentences containing the real words.

Independent Work

Give each group a set of prepared cards from "Add the *e*" (p. 73) and a pencil. Ask children to choose a card and read the word on it. Stress that the vowels in these words will make a short-vowel sound, as there is no silent *e* at the end. Tell children to add silent *e* to the end of each word and read the new word created. Stress that the vowel will now make a long-vowel sound because silent *e* has changed the sound it makes. Challenge children to decide whether the word created is a real word or not. Tell them to list the words under the headings "real words" or "not real words." Encourage them to share their lists with a talking partner and resolve any differences of opinion through discussion.

Give less-confident learners only those words containing one of the vowels. Challenge more-confident learners by asking them to put the real words created into sentences instead of just listing them.

Wrap-Up

Discuss and compare the words created during independent work. Show page 6 of the Notebook file and ask children to name the objects. Challenge them to spell each of the words on individual whiteboards, then ask one child to come up to the SMART Board to write the word on screen in the space provided. Once they have done this, use the Eraser from the Pen tray to reveal the correct answer. Assess and review children's responses. Repeat the same activity on page 7.

Reading Nonfiction

Learning objectives

- To recognize the main elements that shape different texts.
- To convey information in simple non-narrative forms.
- To compose and write simple sentences independently to communicate meaning.

Resources

- "Reading Nonfiction" Notebook file
- "Finding Answers" (p. 74)
- pencils

(Microsoft Power-Point is required to view the embedded slideshow in the Notebook file.)

Whiteboard tools

- Pen tray
- Select tool
- Highlighter pen

Getting Started

Go to page 2 of the "Reading Nonfiction" Notebook file. Ask: *What is a nonfiction book?* (A book that gives some sort of information to the reader) Discuss what would normally be on the front cover of a nonfiction book and look at some examples. Ask: *What would you normally find at the front of a nonfiction book?* Encourage children to explain the purpose of the contents page and how it can be used to find information. Write any key words on page 2.

Mini-Lesson

1. Go to page 3 of the Notebook file and open the electronic book.

2. Show the front cover to children and ask them to give the title of the book. Ask what type of book they think it is and what it might be about.

3. Explain that to turn the pages of the book they must press the arrows at the bottom of the pages.

4. Suggest looking on the next page to find out more about the content of the book.

5. Confirm that the book is a nonfiction book about insects and then read the book as a class. Discuss the text as you read it.

6. Explain that the book doesn't need to be read in order and that by pressing on the hyperlinks on the contents page you can move straight to that page.

7. Ask children some simple questions about the book. Encourage them to go straight to the page that the answer is on and highlight the relevant part of the text.

8. When children have finished exploring the electronic book, press Escape on your keyboard to exit the slideshow.

Independent Work

Provide each child with a copy of "Finding Answers" (p. 74). Ask children to read the first paragraph quietly to themselves. Explain that the questions can be answered using information found in that paragraph. Support children in writing an answer to each of the questions. Encourage them to write in full sentences if possible. Tell them to complete the rest of the sheet in the same way, by reading the next paragraph then answering the questions beneath it.

Less-confident learners should work with an adult, who can read the paragraphs and questions aloud to them while they follow on their own sheets. Encourage more-confident learners to write a paragraph of their own and make up some questions for it.

Wrap-Up

Look at the questions together as a class and solicit answers from a range of children. Evaluate which answers were given in sentences and who gave the most accurate answers. Page 4 of the Notebook file can be used for assessment purposes. Encourage children to make up their own questions that can be answered using the information on the reproducible sheet. Invite the rest of the class to answer these invented questions.

Listening to Narratives

Learning objectives

- To initiate conversation, attend to, and take account of what others say.
- To interact with others, negotiating plans and activities and taking turns in conversation.

Resources

- "Listening to Narratives" Notebook file
- photographs from home
- tape recorder

Whiteboard tools

- Pen tray
- Select tool

Getting Started

Initiate a sharing session with children. Ask: *What did you do over the weekend? Did anyone play games? Did anyone go to a party?*

Allow children time to take turns talking about what they have done. Support the discussion with appropriate questions and responses. Ask: *Why? Where? When?* Encourage children to also ask questions. Write down their comments on page 2 of the "Listening to Narratives" Notebook file.

Mini-Lesson

1. Look at the picture on page 3 of the Notebook file. Ask: *What do you think the girl is doing?* Press on the picture to hear the girl talk. Repeat the description if necessary.

2. Ask questions such as: *What did the girl do? Why did she go to bed? Do we know when she went to bed? What do you think happened next?*

3. Go on to look at the pictures on pages 4 and 5 and listen to the narrative. Discuss with children what they know and what they don't know about what the child is doing. For example, on page 4: *What is the girl going to wear? What did she say?*

4. Encourage children to focus on what they have heard, rather than what they think they know.

5. Move to page 6. Ask: *What is happening in the picture?* Help them record the narrative that might go with the picture. For example: *The boy is playing with his train set.* Suggest that they give some more information. For example: *The boy is playing with his train set because he likes trains.* Support children as they work through pages 6 to 8, recording what they think the children might be doing in each picture.

Independent Work

At another session, ask children to bring in photographs from home. Invite them to talk about the pictures with a partner. Model some questions to support their narration of the experiences. Ask: *Where were you? When did this happen? Who were you with?* Encourage other children to listen and ask questions. Allow time for thinking and for children to frame their ideas in words.

Wrap-Up

Go to page 9 of the Notebook file. Ask: *What is happening in the picture? What do you think the boy is doing?* Listen to the sound recording. Decide which picture the little girl is talking about. Ask: *Why do you think it is this one? What can you see in the picture? What did you hear?* Repeat the activity on page 10.

Writing Captions

Learning objectives
- To use writing as a means of recording and communicating.
- To attempt writing for different purposes.
- To write things such as labels and captions.

Resources
- "Writing Captions" Notebook file
- "Captions" (p. 75)
- cardboard and other materials for children to make models of buildings
- small action figures
- large rectangular and square shapes
- digital camera
- paper
- writing, drawing, and coloring materials

Whiteboard tools
- Pen tray
- Delete button
- Select tool
- On-screen Keyboard
- Text tool

Getting Started

Open page 2 of the "Writing Captions" Notebook file. Tell children that in this part of the lesson you are going to look at and talk about the photographs on the Notebook pages, then read the captions that go with them.

Look at the first photograph together. Ask: *What kind of building or store do you think this is?* Invite children to think of a caption that they would put with this photograph. Next, use the Delete button to remove the green box on the screen to reveal the prepared sentence underneath. Press on the text to hear the sentence read aloud. Is it similar to children's idea? *Why is this a sentence?* (It has a period and capital letter.) Ask: *Why is this sentence helpful?* (It tells the readers what type of store appears in the photograph.) Repeat this activity for the photographs on pages 3 and 4.

Mini-Lesson, Part 1

1. Reread the sentence on page 2 of the Notebook file. Tell children that the sentence is too short and that they need to add some extra information. Invite them to consider what else can be added to make a longer caption for the picture. Ask: *What else can we tell people about the flower shop?*

2. Give children time to talk to a partner to think of some ideas for the photographs on pages 2 to 4.

3. Listen to a range of suggestions and use page 5 to write down children's ideas.

4. Together, decide upon the best ideas and return to pages 2 to 4. Scribe the rest of each sentence (choose a different color).

5. Complete at least two captions for each photograph.

Mini-Lesson, Part 2

1. Display page 6 of the Notebook file. Press on the text to hear the sentence read aloud. Say: *We need to write another sentence to tell people what this building is used for.*

2. Scribe children's extra sentences for them on the Notebook page (in different colors). Complete at least one sentence for the photographs on pages 6 to 8.

3. Give children copies of "Captions" (p. 75). Ask them to talk in groups about the pictures displayed and to suggest captions for each picture. If available, ask another adult to support the groups by scribing these captions onto the sheet.

4. Encourage older or more-confident learners to try to write the sentences for the captions themselves.

5. In subsequent sessions, provide children with paper, pens, and some square and rectangular shapes. Help them draw a square shape to make a box for a picture and use a rectangular shape for a caption.

6. Ask children to use a digital camera to take a photograph and supply a caption to go with it.

(continued)

Independent Work

Set up a learning center containing cardboard, recycled materials, and other materials for children to make buildings, with paper and pens available for children to write labels or signs for the buildings. (If necessary, ask an adult to help children write the labels.) Invite children to talk about who works and lives in the different buildings they have made.

Wrap-Up

Review the completed Notebook file and reproducible pages. Ask children to reread the sentences they have written about the buildings. Point out that the captions now contain more than one sentence. Together, read out just the first sentence for one of the captions. Ask: *How will we know when to stop reading? How do we know it is the end of the sentence?* Remind children that they have produced more than one sentence and that together these sentences form a caption.

Greeting Cards

Learning objectives

- To know that information can be relayed in the form of print.
- To know that print carries meaning.

Resources

- "Greeting Cards" Notebook file
- "Thinking of You" (p. 76)
- collection of greeting cards (or cards children have brought in)
- tissue paper, glue, scissors, colored pencils, and crayons

Whiteboard tools

- Pen tray
- Select tool

Getting Started

Display a collection of greeting cards in the classroom. Invite children to look at and talk about the cards. Then give each pair or small group of children one card to look at. Ask: *Who do you think might like a card like this? What do you think the card is for? When do you receive cards? When do you send cards?*

Encourage children to explain their answers using the word *because*. For example: *I think this greeting card is for someone's birthday because there is a cake with candles on the front.*

Mini-Lesson

1. Have a collection of greeting cards available for children to look at.

2. After the initial discussion, open up the greeting cards and ask children to look at the caption text inside. Ask: *What words or letters do you recognize? Can you find the letter that your name begins with? What do you think this might say?*

3. Collect and write a list of the captions or phrases from inside the cards on page 2 of the "Greeting Cards" Notebook file (such as Happy Birthday, Greetings, and Get Well Soon).

Independent Work

Set up a card-making center for children to create their own greeting cards. Provide tissue paper, glue, scissors, colored pencils and crayons, and any other suitable materials for children to use. Show children a copy of "Thinking of You" (p. 76) and talk about the pictures on it. Look at the different characters and decide what sort of card you could send to them. Invite children to tell you what captions might be suitable to go on their cards.

Wrap-Up

Choose some of the cards that children have made. Invite the creators of these cards to stand up and show their cards to the rest of the class. Encourage the other children to explain what they like about one another's cards. Prompt them with questions, such as: *Who do you think this card is for? What does it say inside?* Explain that in the next lesson children will be designing their own greeting cards on the SMART Board.

Go to page 3 of the Notebook file, which displays three pictures and three greetings. Read the three greetings to children. Ask them to consider which greeting would fit with each picture. Invite individual children to explain their answers. Show them how to press on the text and drag and drop each greeting to the matching card.

Writing With Purpose

Learning objectives

- To ascribe meanings to marks.
- To use writing as a means of recording and communicating.
- To write their own names and other things such as labels and captions.

Resources

- "Writing With Purpose" Notebook file
- tissue paper
- glue
- scissors
- colored pencils
- crayons
- old greeting cards
- blank cards
- collage materials (such as shiny paper, sequins, beads, etc.)

Whiteboard tools

- Pen tray
- Select tool
- Delete button
- On-screen Keyboard

Getting Started

Review the previous lesson on greeting cards.

Mini-Lesson, Part 1

1. Display page 2 of the "Writing With Purpose" Notebook file. Explain to children that you would like to send a card to Snow White. Press on each star button on the page to hear the different greetings read aloud.

2. Invite children to decide what sort of greeting they would like to send to Snow White. Ask: *Which message do you think is best? Why?* Encourage children to discuss the various options and to explain their choices.

3. When children have chosen the message, press on the text to go to a page where they can choose an image for the card. Ask them what kind of picture they think Snow White would like.

4. Allow children some opportunity to talk in pairs or small groups and decide on the most suitable picture for the greeting card that you are going to send her. Ask questions such as: *Why do you think Snow White would like that picture? Why do you think this picture would be good for someone who is not feeling well?*

5. When children have chosen an image, press on it to go to a page that contains the final greeting card. (Press on the box in the top right-hand corner of the page to go back to the start and select another greeting card, if you wish.)

Mini-Lesson, Part 2

1. For the next session, work with small groups one at a time and ask children to help you write a personal note to Snow White on the card. Discuss what kind of note would be appropriate in this greeting card.

2. Collate some useful words or phrases on a piece of paper, such as: *Dear, Love from, Best wishes*, and so on.

3. Help children write their message on the SMART Board, using the On-screen Keyboard. Print out the card and then delete the text to prepare for the next group.

Independent Work

Set up a center for children to create their own greeting cards. Supply them with a "treasure box" filled with greeting cards, blank cards, collage materials, shiny paper, sequins, beads, and other treasures. Provide children's names on cards. Encourage them to find their name cards and use them to practice writing their own names. Also provide old greeting cards and captions written on cardstock for children to use when making their own cards. Give them a specific focus for their cards, such as a thank-you card for the cafeteria staff. Allow children some time to write a caption and a message, supporting them if necessary.

Wrap-Up

Share some of the messages from children's homemade greeting cards. Write a collection of words and phrases that have been used on page 31 of the Notebook file. Ask children for suggestions of any other words that could be added to the list.

Sequencing

Learning objectives

- To use vocabulary and forms of speech that are increasingly influenced by experience of books; link statements and stick to a main theme or intention.
- To extend vocabulary, exploring the meanings and sounds of new words.

Resources

- "Sequencing" Notebook file
- "What's the Order?" (p. 77)
- ingredients and tools for making sandwiches
- paper
- glue sticks
- pretend food and kitchen equipment

Whiteboard tools

- Pen tray
- Select tool

Getting Started

Open the "Sequencing" Notebook file and look at the images on page 2. Ask children: *What is happening? What do you think the boy is doing?* Now look at the individual pictures of the boy on pages 3 to 6. Talk about each picture in more detail together. Explain that you would like children to help you write a caption to go with each picture, describing what the boy is doing.

As you go through the pages, ask children to support you as you model the writing to go with each picture. Ask questions such as: *Who can help me remember how to write* the? *What sound can we hear at the beginning of the word* boy?

Occasionally make deliberate mistakes so that children can help you. Invite individuals to come and point to the mistakes on the SMART Board.

Mini-Lesson, Part 1

1. Talk about children's favorite types of sandwich together. Ask them to tell you the ingredients that they think they would need to make their favorite sandwich.

2. Talk about the order in which they might make their sandwich. For example, should they add the filling before the mayonnaise? Should they put the "lid" on the sandwich before they have added the filling?

3. Provide some bread, mayo, and a choice of two or three popular fillings. **(Important note: Check for any food allergies beforehand.)** Help children make a simple sandwich to enjoy at snack time.

4. As you make the sandwiches together, discuss the order in which they are being made. Encourage the use of sequencing vocabulary, such as *next*, *then*, and *to begin with*.

Mini-Lesson, Part 2

1. At the beginning of the next session, remind children of the work you did together, making sandwiches. Invite a volunteer to describe the sequence they followed when making their sandwich.

2. Show children page 7 of the Notebook file. On this page, there are some pictures of the boy making a sandwich.

3. Invite children to help you put the pictures of the sandwich-making in order. Ask: *What should the boy do first?* Facilitate an open discussion: There are many ways to make a sandwich and although some things have to be done in order, there are many variations!

4. Encourage children to think about the sequence of the activity. Invite volunteers to come to the SMART Board and move the pictures into their preferred order. Ask them to describe and justify their sequence.

5. As a class, agree on a sensible order. Discuss the sort of language and vocabulary used to describe the order of events. Encourage children to use words such as *last*, *first*, *next*, *before*, and *after*.

6. Write a list of the useful words on page 8 and read them together.

(continued)

7. Finish the activity with a singing session, using the opportunity to reinforce the sequencing vocabulary. Ask children to spend a few minutes thinking about their bedtime routine. Ask: *What things do you do when you are getting ready for bed?* Invite volunteers to tell you one thing that they do.

8. Write children's ideas on page 9 and read them through together. Decide on an order for the song and move the words into the correct order on the page.

9. Use a well-known tune such as "Here We Go Round the Mulberry Bush" for your song and sing it together. For example: *This is the way we brush our teeth*; *This is the way we put on our pajamas*; *This is the way we read our story*; and so on.

Independent Work

Provide children with copies of "What's the Order?" (p. 77). Invite them to cut out the pictures and decide on the order in which they should go. Provide sheets of paper and glue sticks and suggest that children stick the pictures onto the paper in their chosen sequence. Encourage them to talk about their ideas, justifying their sequences to a partner.

Wrap-Up

Provide pretend food and sandwich-making tools (such as plastic knives and so on) in the dramatic-play area. Allow children to play freely with them. Note whether they use any of the new vocabulary as they are making things for one another in their play. Listen for comments such as: *First, I need some bread...*

Writing Directions

Learning objectives

- To link statements and stick to a main theme or intention.
- To speak clearly and audibly with confidence and control and show awareness of the listener.

Resources

- "Writing Directions" Notebook file
- "Write the Directions" (p. 78)
- paper and pens
- glue sticks
- scissors
- shape templates
- stapler
- hole puncher
- ribbons
- coloring materials

Whiteboard tools

- Pen tray
- On-screen Keyboard
- Select tool

Getting Started

Open the "Writing Directions" Notebook file and look at the images on page 2. Ask: *What do you think is happening? Do you like eating toast? Have any of you helped to make your own toast before?*

Talk to children about what happens when we put bread into the toaster. Ensure that they understand that they should always be with an adult when making toast. Explain that the toaster gets very hot and that the bread, when it comes out of the toaster, is also very hot.

Mini-Lesson

1. Look more closely at the selection of images on page 2 of the Notebook file. Ask: *What is happening? Does the little girl need to follow a special order to make the toast?*

2. Explain that you would like children's help to write some directions to go with each of the pictures.

3. First, invite volunteers to come and help you put the pictures on page 2 in the correct order. At first, make some deliberate and obvious mistakes and encourage children to explain and show you how to correct your errors.

4. Using a Pen from the Pen tray show children how to add numbers to the pictures to show the order.

5. Now go to pages 3 to 7, looking at each picture in order. Discuss each picture in turn, asking children for suggestions of directions to write for each page.

6. Allow children some time to decide what the first direction might be. Use a Pen from the Pen tray or the On-screen Keyboard, accessed through the Pen tray or the SMART Board tools menu, to write down the directions.

Independent Work

Provide each child with a copy of "Write the Directions" (p. 78). Invite children to cut out the pictures from the reproducible page and to think about the order that they might go in. Ask: *Is there more than one way that these pictures could be ordered?* Listen to children's ideas. Provide paper and glue sticks and ask children to glue the pictures in their chosen order. Encourage them to explain their reasons and discuss the order of the pictures as a group. Make sure they use appropriate sequencing vocabulary, such as *first, next, last, finally,* and so on.

Wrap-Up

Teach children an instructional game called "First, Next, and Then." Explain that they can play the game in the classroom, outside, or in an activity area. Tell children that in this game, one child is in charge and must give directions to the other children to follow. In the directions that they give, they must use the words: *First, next, and then.* For example: *First go to the toy box, next choose a toy, and then bring it to me.* Spend some time practicing this order with children (*first, next, and then*). Then let children continue to play in pairs or small groups.

Captions

Learning objective
- To compose and write simple sentences independently to communicate meaning.

Resources
- "Captions" Notebook file
- individual whiteboards and pens (one for each pair)
- display board showing photographs, maps, and drawings of the local area

Whiteboard tools
- Pen tray
- On-screen Keyboard
- Select tool

Getting Started

Talk with children about how they traveled to school this morning and what they saw on the way. Open page 2 of the "Captions" Notebook file, read the captions together, and talk about the pictures on the page. Ask: *Did anyone see any of these things on their way to school? Where did you see them? What were they there for?*

Mini-Lesson

1. Display the pictures and captions on page 3 of the Notebook file. Explain that each picture has two captions, but that the captions are not in order.

2. Read each of the captions carefully with children. Ask them to discuss with a friend which captions go with which pictures.

3. Work with children to match the captions to the pictures. Discuss the choices made.

4. Ask them to think of another caption that could be added to each picture.

5. Put children into mixed-ability pairs and give each pair an individual whiteboard and a pen.

6. Display page 4 and discuss what the picture shows.

7. Ask each pair to decide on a caption that gives some information about the picture. Encourage the more-confident learner in the pair to write the caption on the whiteboard and hold it up for you to see.

8. Share the ideas for captions and discuss children's choices and vocabulary. Invite them to write some of the best captions on the SMART Board, with support.

9. Repeat this activity, using the picture on page 5 of the Notebook file.

Independent Work

Turn children's attention to the prepared display board (see Resources). Discuss all of the different things that are on it. In mixed-ability pairs, ask children to choose the part of the display that they are most interested in and write a caption for it that could be added to the display. Discuss how the work needs to be presented clearly, using a text large enough to be seen from a distance.

Wrap-Up

Share the labels created by each pair with the rest of the class. Ask each pair to add their label to an appropriate position on the display board. Go to page 6 of the Notebook file and evaluate whether the labels are clear to the reader. Praise what is successful and make constructive suggestions for improvements.

Making a List

- To convey information and ideas in simple non-narrative forms.

Resources
- "Making a List" Notebook file
- "How to Make a Fruit Kebab" (p. 79)
- different fruits as listed on page 2 of Notebook file **(Note: Check for food allergies first!)**
- kebab sticks
- plastic knives for children
- sharp knife for teacher or adult assistant

Whiteboard tools
- Pen tray
- Select tool
- On-screen Keyboard

Getting Started

Look at a selection of real fruits and name them. Open page 2 of the "Making a List" Notebook file and match each real fruit to its picture. Read the fruit name labels, then challenge children to add the correct label to each fruit by dragging and dropping the words at the bottom of the page. Explain that they are going to use the real fruit to make a fruit kebab but that they must plan it first.

Mini-Lesson

1. Let children taste a piece of banana (be aware of any allergies that they may have). Encourage them to describe the taste of the fruit, using words such as *sweet*, *soft*, *smooth*, and so on.

2. Use a Pen from the Pen tray to write a list of some of the describing words on page 3 of the Notebook file.

3. Repeat this with the orange.

4. Discuss how the lists are set out down the page, with each new describing word on a new line. Point out that the lists are not written in sentences.

5. Comment that a list would be really useful when planning the fruit kebab, to record which fruit children want to use.

6. Use page 4 to demonstrate how to make a list of fruit. Use the word bank to support spelling.

7. Stress that directions are not always given using words. On page 5, demonstrate how to create a diagram of the kebab by dragging and dropping the fruit images onto the kebab stick.

8. Suggest that children might want to consider how the finished kebab will look when making the list. Ask: *What colors and tastes will be good together? Will the fruit make a pattern?* Go back and forth between pages 4 and 5 to support this.

Independent Work

Give out copies of "How to Make a Fruit Kebab" (p. 79) for children to complete. Explain that they need to complete the list of fruit and then create a labeled diagram of the kebab. Supply a word bank of the fruit names to support spelling if necessary.

Provide less-confident learners with more words to help them with this task. Adapt the sheet for more-confident learners by removing the directions so that they can write their own.

Wrap-Up

Look at page 6 of the Notebook file. Read the directions at the bottom of the page together. Ask children to order the directions by pressing on each sentence at the bottom of the page and dragging and dropping it into the correct position in the box above. Talk about how the directions are set out in order, using numbers and beginning with "bossy" words. Support children as they follow their own directions sheet to create their own fruit kebab. Chop harder fruits with the sharp knife if necessary. Each child can ask a friend to evaluate their kebab by looking at and tasting it. Create a list of some of the comments made in the evaluation on page 7 of the Notebook file.

Plurals

Learning objective
- To investigate and learn the spellings of words with s for plurals.

Resources
- "Plurals" Notebook file
- writing notebooks and pencils
- individual whiteboards and pens
- index cards

Whiteboard tools
- Pen tray
- Select tool
- Delete button
- Highlighter pen

Before You Start
Before the lesson, make a set of cards for each group of children, each card depicting more than one of the same object, such as four cats (choose objects where adding an s makes the word plural). Also provide a word bank of the names of the depicted objects (in singular).

Getting Started
Open the "Plurals" Notebook file and look at the pictures on page 2. Identify what each picture shows. Point to one picture at a time and challenge children to write the name of the object on an individual whiteboard. Ask one child to write the word beneath the picture on the SMART Board. Correct any spelling mistakes as necessary.

Mini-Lesson
1. Ask children what they would call more than one girl. Elicit the answer "girls." Ask: *How has the word changed?*

2. Open page 3 of the Notebook file and go through it with children. Explain the term *plural*. Use the Delete button to delete the star to reveal the answer. Point out that an s is added to many words to make them plural.

3. Show children page 4 and point out that they are the same pictures as on page 2, but now there are more than one of each of the objects.

4. Again using individual whiteboards, invite children to write down what each picture is. Remind them that the words should now be plural.

5. More-confident learners could attempt to write the number word to show how many there are of each object.

6. Invite different children to write each word beneath the picture. Point out that the words are spelled the same as before except that an s has been added to the end to make each word plural.

Independent Work
Give each group a set of prepared cards and a word bank (see Before You Start). Talk with children about what is on each card. Explain that the names of the objects are in the word bank to help them spell the words more easily. Ask children to write down exactly what they can see on the card in their notebooks (for example: 5 cats). Remind them again that there is more than one of each object, so the word must be made plural.

Wrap-Up
Put children into pairs. Display page 5 of the Notebook file and ask children to read the words with their partner. Look at each word individually and ask children to make it plural. Invite them to add s to the end of the words to make the spelling correct. Challenge each pair to choose one of the plural words, put it into a sentence, and write the sentence on an individual whiteboard. Invite one pair to write their sentence on the SMART Board. Highlight the use of the s on the end of the word to make it plural.

Design a Superhero

Learning objectives

- To identify characters in stories and find specific information in simple texts.
- To create short simple texts on paper that combine words with images.
- To group written sentences together in chunks of meaning or subject.

Resources

- "Design a Superhero" Notebook file
- superhero comic books (one for each pair)
- paper and pencils

Whiteboard tools

- Pen tray
- Select tool
- On-screen Keyboard

Getting Started

Hand out a superhero comic book to each pair of children. Give them a few minutes to look at it together, then ask different pairs to tell the rest of the class a little bit about the superhero in their comic.

Go to page 2 of the "Design a Superhero" Notebook file and ask children to suggest a superhero. Discuss what the superhero is like, asking questions such as: *What is his/her name? What does he/she look like? What are his/her powers? Who is he/she in "real" life?* Repeat with other superheroes.

Mini-Lesson

1. Ask children to look carefully at the superhero characters on page 3 of the Notebook file. Point out that they won't have seen these characters in a comic—they are "new" superheroes.

2. Read the descriptive sentences at the bottom of the page and tell children that each sentence describes one of the two characters.

3. Invite children to discuss with a partner which sentences describe which character. Then ask volunteers to come to the SMART Board to drag the sentences into the correct boxes.

4. Challenge children to think of other descriptive sentences about each character.

5. Go to page 4. Explain to children that they are going to write a character profile of a superhero. Ask them to decide upon a superhero and write the name on the line provided. Ask a volunteer to come up and draw the superhero in the box.

6. Explain what each of the headings requires. For example, suggest that for "Heroic actions" children could write about a time when the character saved the world. Encourage them to identify sensible phrases and sentences for each heading.

7. Look closely at vocabulary choices. Invite children to improve their ideas where possible by changing or adding words.

Independent Work

Provide each child with paper and pencils. Ask children to invent their own superhero. They should first draw a picture of their "new" superhero and then complete a written description of him/her. Encourage children to consider their vocabulary choices carefully and choose interesting and accurate describing words.

Supply a word bank of useful words to support less-confident learners. Challenge more-confident learners by asking them to write their description, using their own sentences, in a short passage.

Wrap-Up

Go to page 5 of the Notebook file. Invite children to share some of their superheroes with the rest of the class. Evaluate the vocabulary choices made and discuss whether more detail could have been added to the description. Encourage the rest of the class to ask the inventor questions about his or her superhero that he or she must answer. Make notes on the board as appropriate.

Retelling a Story

Learning objectives
- To retell stories, ordering events using story language.
- To write chronological texts using simple structures.

Resources
- "Retelling a Story" Notebook file
- tape recorder and microphone
- paper and pencils
- precut card arrows

Whiteboard tools
- Pen tray
- Select tool
- On-Screen Keyboard
- Blank Page button

Getting Started
Open page 2 of the "Retelling a Story" Notebook file. Press the thumbnail image to go to the electronic storybook "The Three Little Sheep." Read the story with children. Discuss different ways to decode unfamiliar words and encourage children to use these strategies to help them read the text. Talk about what is happening in the story and clarify the main events. Ask: *Does it remind you of another story?* Compare the story to "The Three Little Pigs," making notes on the board.

Mini-Lesson
1. Ask children to recall the opening sentence used in the story (*Once upon a time . . .*). Work with children to list alternative ways of starting this story.

2. Display page 3 of the Notebook file and ask children to look carefully at the illustrations.

3. Invite them to work as a team to rearrange the illustrations so that they tell the story in the correct order.

4. Suggest that they could add a short caption to each illustration to help retell the story in more detail. Ask them to choose an illustration and think of a caption to accompany it.

5. Go to page 4. Invite children to retell the story orally to a partner. Encourage the listening partners to add any omitted details as they listen.

6. Using pages 5 to 15, invite individual children to use the On-screen Keyboard to type a caption next to each picture to add more detail to the pictorial retelling.

7. Share the newly created text as a class and discuss how it could be improved even further.

Independent Work
Look at the correctly ordered illustrations on page 3 of the Notebook file. Explain to children that they will illustrate the main parts of the story. State what these main parts are. Divide the class into groups of ten and assign one main part of the story to each group member. Have each child create an illustration for his or her part of the story and write a caption on a strip of paper and attach it to the illustration. The group members should then bring their work together and arrange it into the correct sequence to retell the story. Supply each group with precut card arrows to help them organize their work. Give each group access to a tape recorder and ask them to record an oral retelling of their story. Suggest that each child retell his or her own part of the story in sequence. State that it is probable that they will put more detail into their oral retelling than they did into their caption.

Wrap-Up
Go to page 16 of the Notebook page. Scan each group's work and then place each child's illustration on a new Notebook page in the correct order. (Use the Blank Page button to add extra pages to the Notebook file.) Share each group's work with the class by playing back the tape recording and moving to the relevant pages in the Notebook file as needed. Invite children to evaluate each group's retelling of the story.

Describing Things

Learning objectives

- To convey information and ideas in simple non-narrative forms.
- To find and use new and interesting words and phrases, including story language.
- To create short, simple texts on paper that combine words with images.
- To compose and write simple sentences independently to communicate meaning.

Resources

- "Describing Things" Notebook file
- "Catalog Page" (p. 80)
- a collection of old toys to be examined and handled by children

Whiteboard tools

- Pen tray
- Select tool
- On-screen Keyboard
- Shapes tool

Getting Started

Make a museum display of the old toys. Choose one toy and invite children to take a close look at it.

Go to page 2 of the "Describing Things" Notebook file. Invite pairs to spend one minute talking about the toy. Ask them to consider what it is, what it does, what it looks like, and what it is made from. Bring the class together to share some of their ideas. Record some of the ideas on the Notebook page.

Mini-Lesson

1. Explain that museums catalog their artifacts so that they have a written record of everything they own.

2. Tell children that they are going to create a catalog of the toys in the class museum.

3. Use pages 3 to 6 of the Notebook file to explore some catalog descriptions of old toys. Read and discuss the phrases. Point out that they give information as a list, using bullet points.

4. Invite children to write a descriptive sentence about the toy at the bottom of the page. They could use one of the phrases as a basis for the sentence, or invent a completely new sentence.

5. Use page 7 to practice writing descriptive phrases that give information about a toy. Look closely at the picture and discuss what it is, what it does, what it looks like, and what it is made from.

6. List some descriptive phrases next to the bullet points. Challenge children to write a simple descriptive sentence about the toy on the line at the bottom of the page.

Independent Work

Give each group of children a few different toys to examine. Allow enough time for the groups to look carefully at the toys and discuss them. Give out copies of "Catalog Page" (p. 80). Ask each child to choose a toy to write about. Children should draw a labeled picture and list some descriptive phrases about the toy. Encourage children to make good vocabulary choices that give clear information about the toy.

Offer a word bank for less-confident learners to help them access technical vocabulary. As an extension, challenge more-confident learners to turn their phrases into a short passage describing the toy.

Wrap-Up

Set out the toys that have been described so that the whole class can see them. Scan some of the catalog descriptions onto page 8, covering the pictures using the Shapes tool. (Insert scanned images by selecting Insert, then Picture File, and browsing to where you have saved the images.) Show each description and challenge children to identify which toy is being described. Ask: *How did you know it was this toy? What could be changed or added to make it clearer which toy is being described?* Work with children to turn one of the lists into a short passage, using capital letters and periods correctly.

Capital Letters

Learning objective
- To use capital letters and periods when punctuating simple sentences.

Resources
- "Capital Letters" Notebook file
- picture book
- index cards
- notebooks and pencils

Whiteboard tools
- Pen tray
- Select tool
- Highlighter pen
- On-screen Keyboard

Before You Start

Prepare a set of cards for each group of students. The cards should feature simple sentences without capital letters.

Getting Started

Open page 2 of the "Capital Letters" Notebook file. Look carefully at the letters and ask children what they notice about them. Focus on the fact that some of the letters are lowercase and some are uppercase (or capital). Invite children to sort the letters into either lowercase or uppercase by selecting them and dragging them to the correct set.

Mini-Lesson

1. Ask children where a capital letter can normally be found.

2. Display page 3 of the Notebook file and explain that a sentence always begins with a capital letter.

3. Comment that the pronoun *I* and the initial letters of people's names are also always capital.

4. Read the sentences on page 4 with children. Explain that they are sentences because they start with a capital letter, end with a period, and make sense on their own.

5. Encourage children to look closely at the sentences to find the capital letters. Invite different volunteers to highlight them.

6. Discuss why the capital letters have been used—for example, the beginning of a sentence, the initial letter of someone's name, the personal pronoun *I*.

7. Show the sentences on page 5 and comment that they are not correct because a robber has stolen all of the capital letters.

8. Invite children to replace the capital letters, explaining why they are needed in each case. Check the answers by pulling the screen across the sentences.

Independent Work

Give each group a set of prepared cards (see Before You Start). Tell children to choose a card and rewrite the sentence in their notebooks with the capital letters in the correct place. Stop children at various points and ask them to check what they have done so far, making sure that each sentence begins with a capital letter.

Work with less-confident learners to find and highlight capital letters in simple sentences. Help them to identify that capital letters are always at the beginning of a sentence. Challenge more-confident learners by asking them to write their own sentences about a given topic, using capital letters where appropriate.

Wrap-Up

Introduce the punctuation game to children. Tell them they are going to read from a picture book, and when they see a capital letter they must put both hands straight up in the air to make themselves tall like a capital letter. Extend the game further by telling them to stab the air with their index finger, as though they are making a period, when they see a period. Read the picture book together at a steady pace and add the actions.

Periods

Learning objective

• To use capital
  letters and periods
  when punctuating
  simple sentences.

Resources

• "Periods"
  Notebook file
• picture book
• paper and pencils
• index cards

Whiteboard tools

• Pen tray
• Select tool
• Highlighter pen
• On-screen
  Keyboard

Before You Start

Before the lesson, prepare a set cards for each group, each card showing two simple, related sentences with the periods omitted. (Make sure that the sentences don't always end at the end of a line.)

Getting Started

Introduce the punctuation game to children. Tell them that you are going to read a picture book story aloud, and when they see a capital letter or period they are going to do an action. For a capital letter, they must put both hands straight up in the air to make themselves tall like a capital letter. For a period, they must stab the air with their index fingers as though they are making a period. Read the picture book story aloud slowly and have them add the actions.

Mini-Lesson

1. Ask: *Where do we find periods?* Go to page 2 of the "Periods" Notebook file. Explain that periods are found at the end of a sentence and are followed by a capital letter, if another sentence follows.

2. Read the sentences on page 3 together. Ask: *Why are these sentences?* (They begin with a capital letter, end with a period, and make sense on their own.)

3. Encourage children to look closely at the sentences to find the periods. Invite them to use a Highlighter pen to highlight them. Point out that the period is always at the end of the sentence.

4. Display page 4. Ask children to identify what is wrong. Invite volunteers to come to the SMART Board to add the missing periods. After all the periods have been added, invite a child to pull the screen from the left-hand side of the page across the text to check the answers.

5. Look at some sentences in the picture book. Find examples where the sentence runs onto the next line of text. Point out that the periods are always at the end of a sentence, but not always at the end of a line. Make this difference very clear.

Independent Work

Give each group a set of prepared cards (see Before You Start). Tell children to choose a card and rewrite it on paper, with the periods in the correct place. Stop children at various points and ask them to check what they have done so far to make sure that each sentence ends with a period.

Wrap-Up

Look at some of the work completed by children and comment on what they have done well. Correct any common mistakes. Look at page 5 of the Notebook page and work as a class to decide where to put the periods in the passage. Add the periods by either using the On-screen Keyboard to type them in or using a Pen from the Pen tray to write them. Keep rereading the text, pausing at the periods already placed, to help children to check their decisions.

Question Marks

Learning objective

- To use capital letters and appropriate end punctuation marks when writing simple sentences.

Resources

- "Question Marks" Notebook file
- half-lined 8-1/2" x 11" paper
- pencils

Whiteboard tools

- Pen tray
- Highlighter pen
- Select tool

Getting Started

Display page 2 of the "Question Marks" Notebook file. Read the sentences together, then look carefully at the initial word and the end of each sentence and ask children what they notice. Conclude that each sentence is a question because it ends with a question mark and begins with a question word. Ask children to highlight the question marks using one color and the question words using another color. Invite them to draw some question marks in the air with their fingers to practice their formation.

Mini-Lesson

1. Ask children to explain how they would identify whether a sentence was a question or a statement.

2. Show children page 3 of the Notebook file. Ask them whether the top sentence (*This sweater is blue.*) is a statement or a question, and invite a volunteer to drag it into the correct box. Get children to sort the rest of the sentences in the same way. Ask them to explain how they know which set each sentence belongs to.

3. Create a collection of question words (for example, *what*, *when*, *how*, *where*) and list them on page 4.

4. Challenge children to think of an example question that begins with each word.

5. Introduce children to the alien from Zog on pages 5 to 7. Encourage them to think of some questions they might like to ask the alien.

6. Invite two children to write their question ideas on page 7. Highlight the capital letter at the beginning of the question word and the question mark at the end.

Independent Work

Give children a piece of half-lined 8-1/2" x 11" paper. Ask them to draw a picture of an alien on the unlined half of the paper. Encourage them to consider what they would like to find out about their alien. Give some examples: *Where are you from? How old are you?* Tell children to write their questions on the lined half of the paper. Remind children regularly that their questions should begin with a capital letter at the start of a question word and end with a question mark.

To simplify the task for less-confident learners, provide the questions on cards, omitting the question marks, and ask children to copy them and add question marks at the end. To extend the task, invite more-confident learners to write a reply to each of their questions. Remind them that the answers will end in a period, not a question mark.

Wrap-Up

Invite a confident child to pretend to be the alien and allow the rest of children to ask their questions. Scribe some of the questions on page 8 of the Notebook file, emphasizing the question words and question marks. Ask children to check their own work to ensure they have included question marks at the end of their questions. Write some of the alien's answers beneath the questions and ask children whether a question mark is needed at the end of them.

Classroom Labels

Wash your hands here.

Hang up your coats here.

Read your book here.

What's In Our Classroom?

Alphabet

a	b	c	d
e	f	g	h
i	j	k	l
m	n	o	p
q	r	s	t
u	v	w	x
	y	z	

Bear Hunt Map

Name

Date

60

Make Your Own Story

Choose some pictures and cut them out.

Circle Game

Use these letters to make new words.

f   a

c   t

n   p

Make Words

Cut out the letters. Put the letters in the frame to spell words.

c	d	t
m	r	n

Rhyming Words

Match the words that rhyme.

dog

van

fish

moon

man

hat

spoon

pin

bat

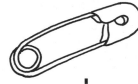

frog

chin

dish

CVC Words

Add the missing letters.

s__n	 ra__	__ot
 cu__	 ma__	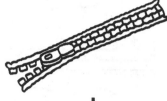 __ip
 __ig	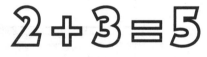 su__	 do__
ca__	 wi__	 __at
 h__t	 __ip	b__g

Color Mixing

Mix some colors! Color the clouds and write in the color words. Use the word bank to help you.

| blue   yellow   brown   purple   orange   red   green |

_____ + _____ = _____

_____ + _____ = _____

_____ + _____ = _____

_____ + _____ = _____

_____ + _____ = _____

Is That a Word?

Sort these words into "real words" and "not real words."

crat	brick
cron	grop
from	trust
prun	press
crab	drep
grin	trab
frass	drip
trim	breg

Pairing Socks

Put the socks in pairs to make words.

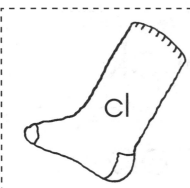 cl

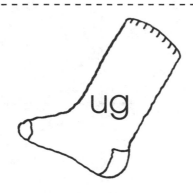 ug

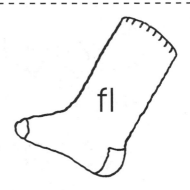 fl

 ob

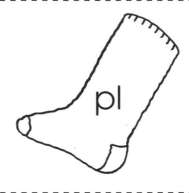 pl

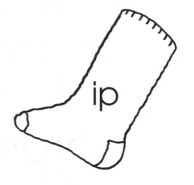 ip

 gl

 um

 sl

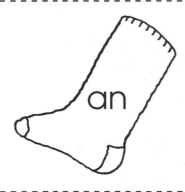 an

 bl

 ot

Bingo Blends

Bingo board 1

st	nk	nt	nd
sk	nk	st	sk
sp	nd	sp	nt

Bingo board 2

nd	nt	sp	nk
st	st	nd	sk
nt	sp	sk	nk

Word cards

rest	ant	tank	gasp
mint	risk	sink	crisp
and	just	wind	went
mask	find	trunk	pink
tusk	wasp	task	mist

ee or *ea*?

Add *ee* or *ea* to these words.
Make sure you choose the correct one!

sh_ _p

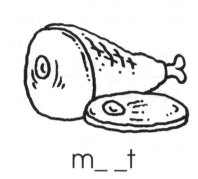

m_ _t

h_ _l

tr_ _

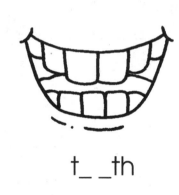

t_ _th

s_ _l

Don likes to f _ _ d the ducks on the pond.

The king had a big f _ _ st and invited all of his friends.

Sometimes I have bad dr _ _ ms at night.

The grass in my garden is gr _ _ n.

Kim's favorite food is vanilla ice cr _ _ m.

Jack climbed up a very tall b _ _ nstalk.

oa or *ow?*

Read the clues and fill in the answers to this crossword.
All of the words have *oa* or *ow* in them.

Across

1. Underneath

3. A big, black bird

6. Shot with a bow

7. Like a frog but bigger

Down

2. Opposite of *high*

4. Cars drive on this

5. Wear this when it is cold

Think of some more words that have *oa* or *ow* in them.

oo, ew, or ue?

Read these sentences. Fill the blanks in the sentences with words from the word bank at the bottom of this page.

I sleep in my _____ .

We use _____ to stick things together.

My sunflower seed _____ very tall.

On a nice day, the sky is _____.

We wear rain _____ when it's raining outside.

The bird _____ up to its nest.

At night, the _____ is in the sky.

A carpenter uses his _____ to do his job.

WORD BANK

blue	tools	moon	boots
grew	flew	bedroom	glue

Add the *e*

cat	tub	rod
win	stop	pin
man	hat	kit
past	van	dip
put	pit	cub
fin	cut	slab
cod	had	not
lost	clip	bun
rob	sum	plot
grim	tap	rip

Finding Answers

Honeybees

A honeybee is an insect. It has six legs and one pair of wings. It has a yellow and black striped body. Honeybees collect nectar from flowers. They make honey from the nectar. People keep honeybees in beehives. They collect honey from the beehives.

Questions

How many legs does a honeybee have?

_____

What does a honeybee look like?

_____

What do honeybees make from nectar?

_____

Where do people keep bees?

_____

Butterflies

A butterfly is an insect. It has six legs and two pairs of wings. Butterflies drink nectar from flowers. They use their long tongues to reach inside the flowers. Butterflies lay eggs. The eggs hatch into caterpillars. The caterpillars eat lots of leaves. Then they turn into butterflies.

Questions

What do butterflies drink?

_____

What do caterpillars eat?

_____

Captions

Write captions for the pictures in the boxes provided.

Thinking of You

What is happening in these pictures?

What's the Order?

Cut out the pictures and put them in order.

Write the Directions

Cut out the pictures. Glue them to paper in the correct order.
Write directions for each picture.

How to Make a Fruit Kebab

What you need:

-
-
-
-
-
-

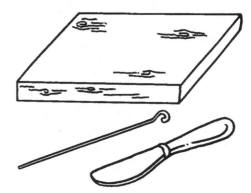

What to do:

Chop the fruit into small pieces.

Put the pieces of fruit on to the kebab stick.

Eat the kebab and enjoy!

Catalog Page

Make a catalog page for an old toy.

```
┌─────────────────────────────────────────┐
│                                         │
│                                         │
│                                         │
│                                         │
│                                         │
│                                         │
│                                         │
└─────────────────────────────────────────┘
```

- _____

- _____

- _____

- _____

Write some sentences about the toy.

_____

_____

_____

_____